Since my youth, O God, you have taught me

and to this day I declare your marvelous deeds.

Even when I am old and gray,

do not forsake me, O God,

till I declare your power to the next generation,

your might to all who are to come.

PSALM *71:17-18*

Wayne Rice

REINVENTING

YOUTH MINISTRY

(AGAIN)

From Bells and Whistles
to Flesh and Blood

IVP Books

An imprint of InterVarsity Press
Downers Grove, Illinois

InterVarsity Press
P.O. Box 1400, Downers Grove, IL 60515-1426
World Wide Web: www.ivpress.com
E-mail: email@ivpress.com

InterVarsity Press® is the book-publishing division of InterVarsity Christian Fellowship/USA®, a movement of students and faculty active on campus at hundreds of universities, colleges and schools of nursing in the United States of America, and a member movement of the International Fellowship of Evangelical Students. For information about local and regional activities, write Public Relations Dept., InterVarsity Christian Fellowship/USA, 6400 Schroeder Rd., P.O. Box 7895, Madison, WI 53707-7895, or visit the IVCF website at <www.intervarsity.org>.

All Scripture quotations, unless otherwise indicated, are taken from the Holy Bible, New International Version®. NIV®. *Copyright ©1973, 1978, 1984 by International Bible Society. Used by permission of Zondervan Publishing House. All rights reserved.*

The lyrics on page 49 are from the song "If I Didn't Have Love," copyright 1976 House of Hits/BMI. Used by permission.

Design: Cindy Kiple
Images: Brendon De Suza/iStockphoto

ISBN 978-0-8308-3313-9

Printed in the United States of America ∞

Library of Congress Cataloging-in-Publication Data

Rice, Wayne.
  Reinventing youth ministry (again): from bells and whistles to flesh and blood / Wayne Rice.
      p. cm.
  Includes bibliographical references.
  ISBN 978-0-8308-3313-9 (pbk.: alk. paper)
  1. Church work with youth. I. Title.
  BV4447.R443 2010
  259'.23—dc22
                                                                          2010014327

| P | 18 | 17 | 16 | 15 | 14 | 13 | 12 | 11 | 10 | 9 | 8 | 7 | 6 | 5 | 4 | 3 | 2 | 1 |
| Y | 25 | 24 | 23 | 22 | 21 | 20 | 19 | 18 | 17 | 16 | 15 | 14 | 13 | 12 | 11 | 10 |

CONTENTS

ACKNOWLEDGMENTS

At the risk of leaving a few people out, let me acknowledge and thank a few friends, colleagues and heroes for their immeasurable contributions to my youth ministry story: Mrs. Laura Baughman, Jerry Riddle, Don Goehner, Sam McCreery, Dave Sheffel, Jim Slevcove, Bob Kraning, Paul Sailhamer, Gary Wilburn, Bufe Karraker, Larry Ballenger, Jerry Anderson, Jay Kesler, Joseph Bayly, Jack Hamilton, Gene French, Ken Overstreet, Jim Green, Tom Goble, Keith Wright, Jack Young, Denny Rydberg, Stan Beard, Tic Long, Craig McNair Wilson, Ben Patterson, Noel Becchetti, E. G. "Von" VonTrutschler, Jim Burns, Rich Van Pelt, Bill McNabb, Ray Johnston, Mark Senter, Tony Campolo, Duffy Robbins, Chap Clark, Dave Veerman, Chuck Workman, Steve Glenn, Dave Grauer, Scott Oas, Craig Knudsen and Ken Elben. Thanks also to Greg Johnson at WordServe Literary Group and Dave Zimmerman at InterVarsity Press for bringing this book to fruition. And a special thanks to College Avenue Baptist Church in San Diego for giving me another shot at youth ministry. I hope I get it right this time.

To my three children, Nathan, Amber and Corey: you have taught me more about life and ministry than you'll ever know. I am so grateful for you and pray that you will continue to love God and serve him in your own unique ways. Nate, thanks for reading this book and giving me the go-ahead to get it published.

And to my wife, Marci, my greatest encouragement and best friend through (so far) forty-four years of ministry together: This story is also your story. Thank you for allowing me to take up so much of our time putting it all into words. I love you so much.

INTRODUCTION

I was introduced at a speaking engagement recently as one of the *inventors* of youth ministry. Whether the youth pastor who introduced me was badly misinformed or just making a joke about my advanced age, I'm not certain. But I had to begin my talk with a bit of a disclaimer: I may *look* old enough to have had Jesus in my youth group but I certainly wasn't around for the invention of youth ministry—whenever that was.

I don't think anybody really knows when youth ministry was invented. It must have been invented by someone however, because there's no specific mention of it in the Bible anywhere—something that has for a long time been problematic for youth pastors trying to justify their job descriptions. And there's not much evidence of youth ministry in early church history either.

Some believe it began with the Sunday school movement in the eighteenth century or the formation of the Christian Endeavor Society around the turn of the twentieth. Some think the birth of youth ministry coincides with the first Youth for Christ rallies in Chicago or the founding of Young Life in the 1940s. And others say it all started in 1525 when Martin Luther shocked his confirmation class of 13-year-olds by pulling out a guitar and doing an impromptu version of his Small Catechism to the tune of "Kum Bah Yah My Lord."[1]

Actually there are hundreds of youth ministry pioneers to whom we owe a debt of gratitude, but I sometimes wonder if any of them would want to take credit for inventing what youth ministry looks like today. While I'm sure they would applaud and encourage today's generation of youth workers, I'm not so sure they would be happy with the results we've been getting of late:

- After more than seventy-five years of youth ministry under our belts, one would expect to find churches more populated with young people than ever before. But churches are losing young people in record numbers.

- With all of the resources we now have at our disposal, one would expect that students would be more firmly grounded in their faith than ever before. But today's teens are less able to articulate what they believe than any generation in history.

- With the incredible amount of money and technology that we now have to reach today's young people with the gospel, one would expect to find an increasing number of teenagers coming to Christ. But more young people today have a negative opinion of Christianity than at any time in recent memory.[2]

I'm not going to repeat here all the bad news and negative statistics that have surfaced lately about the ineffectiveness of youth ministry. Suffice it to say youth ministry is going through something of a midlife crisis. Youth workers are trying to figure out how to attract and keep teenagers engaged in their youth ministry programs. The ideas and structures of the past just aren't working all that well anymore. Some of the most popular youth ministry models are being called into question. What are we doing wrong? Has youth ministry become counter-productive? Is it time for the abolishment of youth ministry?

Some people think it's time to pull the plug, but I'm not one of them. It's not youth ministry's fault that we're losing so many kids. Truth is, we're not living in Mayberry anymore. The world has changed a lot in the last few years, not to mention the needs, preferences and attitudes of young people. We live in a much more secularized, postmodern world. We've never before had to deal with a culture which is so hostile to Christianity and the church. There are many forces working against us these days. While youth ministry may serve as a convenient scapegoat, it is not the culprit here.

If anything, youth ministry has had a more positive than negative impact on the young people today who profess faith in Christ. I hate to think what those numbers would be if youth ministry had *not* been invented. There's no question that many churches are doing a better job meeting the needs of kids than they ever have before. I have nothing but praise and admiration for the vast majority of men and women who are working with young people in the church today.

I believe God called modern-day youth ministry into existence. As the world began to isolate and exploit the teen population, God raised up an army of youth workers to come alongside young people, treat them with respect and speak truth into their lives. Youth ministry may not be perfect and may have a long way to go, but God didn't make a mistake by calling the quarter-million-plus adults who are serving in church youth ministries right now. You can bet that he'll be calling a lot more in the future. God has gifted the church with the people and resources to do more and better youth ministry now than ever before. Youth ministry is still a relatively young enterprise in the history of the church, and it continues to be a work in progress. Obviously there are problems to solve, but we can't give up on youth ministry. We just need to make a few adjustments—

some of them radical—so that we'll be able to become more effective in the future and better stewards of the time, energy and resources we are giving to it.

Maybe you're content with youth ministry just the way it is. I know many youth pastors who wouldn't change a thing. They have thriving youth ministries (at least by most people's standards) and they are getting the kinds of results that parents and church leaders want. Kids are showing up in sufficiently large numbers, the youth ministry programs seem to be humming right along, and the kids are responding—showing up, making decisions, going on trips and behaving themselves. There may be a few hassles, but otherwise life is good.

Fair enough. But hopefully you're not so content with the status quo that you won't be open to some new ways of thinking about youth ministry which aren't really all that new. I sometimes think of my approach to youth ministry as "youth ministry in reverse" because it's really an attempt to address some bad habits that we've picked up over the past fifty years.

I have to admit that I sometimes grow a little bit nostalgic for the days when little old ladies with their hair in buns taught flannel-graph lessons to junior high kids in the church basement. There was something very right about all those adult volunteers who had no idea what they were doing but took turns leading the youth, making sure they were getting their Bible stories straight. It didn't matter that they weren't cool or all that entertaining. They just loved the youth of the church and felt compelled to take responsibility for making sure the young people were becoming firmly grounded in their faith and connected to their church family.

But this isn't a book that idealizes the past. I'm convinced that that today's youth ministry is in most ways superior to what was done in the past. Resources are better and more plentiful, youth workers are more dedicated, better educated and incredibly gifted, programs are built around well-thought-out statements of mission and purpose, and churches provide more and better support for youth ministries than ever before. There is much to commend and recommend about the kind of youth ministry that is being done today.

Years ago I saw a cartoon which pictured two teenagers sitting in the sun, both of them wearing their ball caps backwards. One of them said to the other, "Somebody ought to invent a cap that would give a guy some shade." Something like that is what this book is all about. There's no need to throw out everything we've been doing and start over. Maybe we just need to turn things around a little bit. There's a lot we can learn from the past in order to build onto the present and into the future.

One of the great things about getting old is that the older you get, the more experiences and memories you have from which to draw insight and wisdom. Memories are a real gift from God and I hope I never get so old or forgetful that I can no longer remember all the wonderful things that God has done for me or through me over the years.

So with that in mind, I share with you my youth ministry story along with some observations and recommendations, which I hope you will find enlightening and perhaps applicable to what you're doing now. Keep in mind that my story is only a small slice of the entire youth ministry story, one person's experience and point of view. Much of this story has to do with the early years of Youth Specialties and the relationship I had for many years with my good friend and business partner Mike Yaconelli. Mike tragically died several years ago, and I know that he would likely tell this story with an altogether different slant. I dedicate this book to his memory and the legacy that he left for all of us by telling my story as honestly and candidly as I can.

1

A LONG NIGHT IN CHICAGO
Thinking About Parents

I just wanted to go home.

It was Saturday night, day three of the 1994 National Youth Workers Convention in Chicago, and my responsibilities were essentially over. I led music (it was called "music" back then, not "worship") for three general sessions, taught a couple of seminars and had nothing else to do. Under normal circumstances, I would have been involved in the banquet that was taking place later in the evening and the closing communion service on Sunday morning. But this was not a normal year. I packed my suitcase and headed for the airport, trying not to be noticed as I made my escape through the lobby of the Hyatt Regency Hotel. I really didn't want to explain to anyone why I was leaving the convention early.

As it turned out, no flights were available that night. I tried getting on a couple of standby flights to San Diego, but no luck. Not wanting to return to the convention (which would have meant checking back into the Hyatt) I booked a room at the airport Hilton to wait for my flight the next morning. This turned out to be one of the loneliest nights of my life.

What am I doing here? My thoughts were turning very dark as

I sat there on the bed in front of a flickering hotel room television set. *There's a youth workers convention going on not far from here. I should be there, doing what I do best. I should be leading songs, introducing speakers, leading seminars, talking shop with attendees or catching up with some of my old friends and colleagues. I should be feeling the exhilaration and excitement that always comes from these conventions. Instead, here I am sitting in a stale-smelling hotel room at O'Hare airport feeling awful.*

What I was really feeling was a horrible sense of loss. Only two weeks had passed since Mike Yaconelli and I signed the papers officially terminating our partnership of more than twenty-five years. I was sitting there alone in that hotel room because I was no longer part of Youth Specialties, the company I had cofounded.

Our split-up had been difficult, something like what I imagined a divorce must be like. After so many years of working together, building a business (and ministry) together, writing books together, traveling around the world together, vacationing with our families together, laughing and crying together, Mike and I ended our relationship communicating through lawyers and putting each other through an enormous amount of pain and hurt.

We had been more than business partners, more than friends. Mike and I were like brothers who knew and loved each other so well that squabbles were frequent but usually resolved in a day or two. We were two very different people with different gifts and personalities, but we complemented each other in a yin-yang sort of way. Our odd-couple relationship had served us very well over the years as we accomplished together what neither one of us could have accomplished on our own.

Started on a whim, our little enterprise had grown to become one of the largest providers of youth ministry training and resources in the world. Who would have predicted that two guys with as little business experience as us (none) could create an organization that would last more than twenty-five days, let alone twenty-five years? We did our best to screw it up on many occasions, but somehow God kept his hand on Youth Specialties and blessed it beyond anything that we had ever dreamed or imagined. Mike and I always had a sense that something bigger than us was going on and we were just happy to be along for the ride.

But now it was over—at least it was for me. It felt like a big part of me had just died. So much of my identity, my work and my relationships had been wrapped up in Youth Specialties. The reality that the rest of my life would not include YS was just beginning to sink in.

What was I going to do now? I really wasn't sure. My immediate plans were to start a new ministry for parents. I had created a parenting seminar for Youth Specialties, Understanding Your Teenager, that never quite got off the ground. I loved doing those seminars, however, and my plan going forward was to help parents not just through seminars but through other resources as well.

But I wasn't leaving just to do parent seminars. The truth is that after twenty-five years, I simply had to get away from what had become an enormous source of stress in my life. I loved my work, but I was exhausted and struggling through frequent bouts of anxiety and depression. I don't think many people understood what I was going through (including me) because Youth Specialties appeared to be doing quite well at the time. Our three National Youth Workers Conventions, including this one in Chicago, had overflow crowds. Earlier that year, our National Resource Seminar for Youth Workers had been presented in a hundred cities with more than twenty thousand attendees. We were publishing two magazines, *The Door* and *Youthworker*

Journal, and a monthly newsletter called *Youthworker Update.* New titles were being steadily added to our growing line of youth ministry resources, and our *Ideas Library* was on the bookshelf of just about every youth worker in the country. On the surface, Youth Specialties looked pretty healthy.

But I was miserable, and my relationship with Mike was becoming strained.

I'm not sure when things started going downhill between the two of us. It might have been in 1981 when Mike moved up to Yreka, a small town in northern California, more than eight hundred miles away. A small church in Yreka invited Mike to come and be their pastor, and to everyone's surprise, Mike said yes, packed up his family and was gone. While I thought it was a crazy thing for him to do (especially since the church couldn't pay him anything), it really wasn't any crazier than a lot of things I've known him to do over the years. I tried to be supportive, but I admit I had some resentment that I was left with all the responsibility for overseeing the day-to-day operation of Youth Specialties. We didn't have the Internet, email, cell phones or even fax machines in those days, so the concept of working from a home office didn't make as much sense as it does now. Along with some logistical challenges, Mike's move to Yreka resulted in a good deal of miscommunication between us.

And then came the economic recession of the late 1980s. It wasn't severe, as recessions go, but it almost put Youth Specialties out of business. We were trying to grow a little too fast and discovered we had bitten off more than we could chew. In the spring of 1988 we were conducting more than two hundred events all over North America. We were keeping the airlines busy, working our staff half to death, and losing (we discovered a little too late) a lot of money. Our attendance numbers at those events didn't meet expectations and we found ourselves unable to pay bills or meet payroll. Our bank wouldn't loan us money because we were too far in debt and they didn't understand what kind of business we were in. We could never quite explain Youth Specialties to people who wore suits and ties. Mike and I both tried to scrape together as much money as we could. I mortgaged my house to cover several months' payroll and pay a few bills.

We thought things were improving financially in the fall of 1989 when disaster number two happened. We were just getting our National Youth Workers Convention in San Francisco underway when we heard a rumble and felt the ground move. I was leading a seminar on the second floor of the Hyatt Regency Hotel when the building began to shake violently. Having been in earthquakes before, I casually remarked to the room full of youth workers, "Welcome to California," thinking that the shaking would stop soon enough—but it only continued and got worse. It didn't take long for everyone to realize that this was no ordinary earthquake. We all headed for the exits, wondering if we would make it out of the building alive.

Outside the hotel we learned that what became known as the Loma Prieta earthquake had done extensive damage to the Bay Area's infrastructure and taken many lives. It stopped the third game of the World Series at nearby Candlestick Park and it also canceled our convention. We were just grateful to be alive and realized that our problems were small compared to what many people were going through at that time. But we found ourselves facing more than a quarter million dollars in expenses and refunds. We had no insurance to cover natural disasters and were it not for the generosity of friends, churches and other ministries who believed in us and donated some money, we wouldn't have remained in business.

Youth Specialties survived, but we had to make some hard

decisions. We did what most businesses do when they are having financial trouble—we looked for ways to cut expenses. That December we decided to discontinue several of the events that we had rolled out the previous year. We dropped Grow For It, a one-day seminar for high school students, as well as On the Edge for junior highers. They were terrific events, but we could no longer afford to produce them.

We also decided to do away with an incredible weeklong summer conference that we had produced that year for high school students. It was unlike any student event I've been involved with before or since. The brainchild of Todd Temple, our inaugural Riptide event was held in August 1989 on the campus of Point Loma Nazarene University in San Diego. The event was designed to involve students in a completely new way. Rather than treating them as consumers of a conference program, high school students were invited to actually help create and present the program as it unfolded each day. We brought in an impressive lineup of professional Christian artists and speakers, but they were not there to perform or speak. Instead, they were there to teach the students to do what they do. For example, our faculty included Steve Taylor, a chart-topping Christian artist at the time, who patiently coached several groups of teenagers with rock-star ambitions to perform at our evening meetings while he shouted out encouragement from the sidelines. I'll never forget watching my sixteen-year-old son Nate playing his guitar and singing "Pass It On" to the tune of Iron Butterfly's "In-A-Gadda-Da-Vida." Likewise several young preachers nervously proclaimed God's Word to their peers while coach Tony Campolo sat in the audience shouting "Preach it!" It was a marvelous event, a huge success in terms of accomplishing its mission, but we lost forty grand on it. Adios, Riptide.

Also on the chopping block was Understanding Your Teenager. I had invested two years of development into these seminars and they were beginning to get some traction. I really didn't want us to discontinue them. More than five thousand parents attended our seminars in 1989, but according to our accountants, that wasn't enough.

After the recession ended, Youth Specialties recovered in a surprisingly short period of time. The second mortgage on my house got paid off and we were back making money again. Attendance was good at all of our events. We were turning out some great new products and resources for youth workers and we growing once again. But the stress continued and I was unhappy. Somehow I felt like we were just going through the motions at YS, doing more or less the same things each year. I had several new projects I wanted us to pursue but they all seemed stuck. Mike and I weren't communicating with each other very well any more. There were more stalemates than compromises and more arguments, hurt feelings and lost productivity. What had once been a complementary pairing of two very different personalities had become a frequent source of conflict and dysfunction in our company.

When Mike and I started Youth Specialties, we chose to set it up as a business rather than nonprofit ministry. We made that decision for two reasons. First, we wanted the freedom that came from owning our own business. We simply didn't want to have to ask a board of directors for permission every time we needed to make a decision. Second, we believed in a free-market economy. If we produce goods and services of high quality, customers will pay for them. If we don't, they won't. Rather than asking people to donate money to support us while we produce things nobody wants, we preferred the built-in accountability of a business model that requires a profit to establish viability.

At least that was our thinking. Ironically, we didn't operate under those rules. There were quite a few things we produced at Youth Specialties over the years which never made any money at all, among them *The Wittenburg Door*, which we had published since 1971, and which had never made a dime. And anyway, we didn't really have the freedom we thought we would have as owners of a business. As Youth Specialties grew and became more corporate, we appointed an executive team made up of department heads and gave them the authority to make most of our operational decisions. They were, in effect, our board of directors.

So when the recession hit and our executive team decided to discontinue Understanding Your Teenager, Mike and I could have overridden the decision, but we could never reach agreement on that. We tried to get unstuck on this and other disagreements by hiring a management consultant who put us through a regimen of marathon meetings, interviews and personality tests. He led us through the writing of new mission statements and corporate policy manuals. It was all helpful, but the net result was an added layer of bureaucracy which only seemed to add fuel to our frustration and stress.

We tried counseling. But after several weekly sessions, our counselor gave up and refused to see us anymore. I'm sure he needed therapy himself after all that we put him through.

We went on a spiritual retreat, spending a week in Canada with the renowned priest and author Henri Nouwen. While this was a life-changing experience for all of us, some of our corporate dysfunction spilled over into our retreat experience and spoiled part of our time with Henri. I have a feeling that after we left, he could have written a new book called *The Wounded Healer Meets Abbott and Costello*.

We tried selling the company, thinking that someone else

could run Youth Specialties better than we could. We entertained offers from several well-known publishing companies who expressed interest in acquiring YS, but ultimately we left all of them standing at the altar. We could never agree on how much Youth Specialties was worth or whether to sell at all.

We considered dividing Youth Specialties into two separate companies—with Mike running one half and me the other—but something didn't seem right about that either. King Solomon, two mothers and a baby came to mind.

In the end, I made the decision to sell my interest in Youth Specialties to Mike. My plan was to take the proceeds of the sale and invest it in our Understanding Your Teenager seminars. That's what I really wanted to do full time. But I was feeling a good deal of seller's remorse as I sat there alone in that airport hotel room. As difficult as the last few years had been, I was going to miss working with my old friend Mike and I must say that I miss him still.

THINKING ABOUT PARENTS

I'm not sure when I first took an interest in parent ministry. It was probably about the same time my son Nathan became a teenager, in 1985. He was a great kid but I discovered that I was a lousy parent. I caught myself saying all the dumb things I swore I'd never say to my kids, worrying myself sick over what I should have known was normal behavior and getting angry—both at him and myself—several times a day.

It didn't take long for me to learn that working with other people's kids is a whole lot different than raising your own. All of my considerable knowledge, performance and management skills, accumulated over two decades of youth ministry, were suddenly useless—or at least they seemed that way. I knew I needed help.

At the time Youth Specialties had no resources to offer youth workers on how to help parents or relate to them in any meaningful way. We more or less built our youth ministries on an understanding of adolescence and developmental psychology which assumed teenagers were separating (or had already separated) from their parents. We youth workers were heroically stepping into the gap, becoming the last line of defense between teenagers and the negative influence of friends and entertainment media. We pretty much treated teenagers as if they didn't have parents—or as if their parents were problems, obstacles to overcome. The only thing we really needed or wanted from parents was a little gratitude and, of course, their continued financial support.

Around that time new research was coming out that revealed the enormous influence parents have on the spiritual and moral development of teenagers. (Almost everybody wants to know how to influence teens—especially when it comes to how they spend their money.) Since then even more research has been done. I must say that as a career youth ministry guy I've been looking for some of that research to finally give some props to all of us dedicated youth workers who have tried so diligently over the years to be positive influences on teenagers. No such luck. We keep getting pretty much the same results time after time: for guidance and direction—not only for their faith and values, but for just about everything—teenagers turn first to their parents. Researcher Christian Smith summed it up pretty well:

> Contrary to popular misguided cultural stereotypes and frequent parental misperceptions . . . the evidence clearly shows that the single most important social influence on the religious and spiritual lives of adolescents is their parents. . . . The best social predictor, although not a guaran-

tee, of what the religious and spiritual lives of youth will
look like is what the religious and spiritual lives of their
parents do look like.[1]

What we now know is that teenagers pretty much follow in
the faith footsteps of their parents. If parents are following Jesus, there's a good to excellent chance their kids will follow
Jesus too. If they aren't, they won't. There are no guarantees, of
course, but parents function as the spiritual leaders in their
home whether they want to or not. That's their role, given to
them by God.

Most children experience God by the way their parents connect with them and relate to them. Certainly that's one of the
reasons why God describes himself so often in the Bible as a
loving Father. If we have an earthly father who demonstrates
love, grace and mercy to us, we are likely to have an easier time
understanding God's love, grace and mercy. I can't tell you how
many young people I've known over the years who find it impossible to believe in a God who is interested in them and wants
to listen to them simply because their parents have never set
that example for them at home.

I have all the respect in the world for youth workers in the
church, but I've become more and more convinced over the
years that God never gave to youth workers the responsibility
for making disciples of other people's kids. I realize that's a
point of view that doesn't go over very well with the board of
elders, but it's a truth that is based entirely on Scripture and
reinforced by centuries of Christian practice. God gave that responsibility to parents, not to the local church or the youth
ministry. Sure, there are times when we have to become surro-
gate parents and do some remedial disciple-making in the ab-
sence of willing or capable parents, but the responsibility for

raising kids in the faith has always rested squarely on the shoulders of parents.

But what about the Great Commission? Aren't we commanded to make disciples by Jesus himself (Matthew 28:18-20)? That's true, but Jesus here is commissioning his followers to make disciples of *all the nations*. That's what made the Great Commission so stunning and revolution-

> God never gave to youth workers the responsibility for making disciples of other people's kids.

ary: now the story of God's redemptive love is to be taken to the whole world, not just to the Jews.

Before there was a Great Commission, there was a First Commission—which every Jew was familiar with because it was recited in the *Shema* every single day: "Hear, O Israel: The LORD our God, the LORD is one. Love the LORD your God with all your heart and with all your soul and with all your strength" (Deuteronomy 6:4-5). Along with the command to love God completely was an additional command—a *commission,* if you will—for the propagation of true faith from one generation to the next: "These commandments that I give you today are to be upon your hearts. Impress them on your children. Talk about them when you sit at home and when you walk along the road, when you lie down and when you get up" (Deuteronomy 6:6-7). In these verses God gave parents the commission to teach their children, so that their children would in turn teach their grandchildren and so on down the line.

We can assume that in issuing the Great Commission, Jesus is not rescinding the First Commission in any way but rather amending it, just as he did in Mark 12:31 when he added "and love your neighbor as yourself." The Great Commission is indeed great because it is missional in nature—that is, it opened up the preaching of the gospel to the whole world, not just to the Jews. But from the book of Genesis forward, it's clear that the Bible teaches us that God's plan is for faith to be passed on from one generation to the next—from parents to their children—one family at a time.

- For I have chosen [Abraham], so that he will direct his children and his household after him to keep the way of the Lord. (Genesis 18:19)

- Only be careful, and watch yourselves closely so that you do not forget the things your eyes have seen or let them slip from your heart. . . . Teach them to your children and to their children after them. Remember the day you stood before the LORD . . . when he said to me, "Assemble the people before me to hear my words so that they may learn to revere me as long as they live in the land and may teach them to their children." (Deuteronomy 4:9-10)

- These commandments that I give you today are to be upon your hearts. Impress them on your children. Talk about them when you sit at home and when you walk along the road, when you lie down and when you get up. Tie them as symbols on your hands and bind them on your foreheads. Write them on the doorframes of your houses and on your gates. (Deuteronomy 6:6-9)

- He decreed statutes for Jacob and established the law in Israel, which he commanded our forefathers to teach their children, so that the next generation would know them, even the children yet to be born, and they in turn would tell their children. (Psalms 78:5-6)

- Fathers, do not exasperate your children; instead, bring them up in the training and instruction of the Lord. (Ephesians 6:4)

These and many other passages throughout the Old and New Testaments make it clear that God's plan for the instruction of children in the faith begins in the home.

We get a short glimpse into Jesus' adolescence in Luke 2, where we can see the important role his parents played in his development as a young man. "Then he went down to Nazareth with them [his parents] and was obedient to them. . . . And Jesus grew in wisdom and stature, and in favor with God and men" (Luke 2:51-52). As an adolescent, Jesus put himself under the authority and instruction of Mary and Joseph—his earthly parents—and the results speak for themselves. Scripture allows us to make that connection.

George Barna sums it up pretty well:

> The responsibility for raising spiritual champions, according to the Bible, belongs to parents. The spiritual nurture of children is supposed to take place in the home. Organizations and people from outside the home might support those efforts, but the responsibility is squarely laid at the feet of the family. This is not a job for specialists. It is a job for parents.[2]

WHAT PARENTS BRING

There's really not a lot of debate these days about the power of parents to shape the spiritual lives of their kids, but things haven't changed that much in the way many churches do youth ministry. Most churches still believe that if they just make the right hire and bring in a highly qualified youth pastor with all the training and experience the job demands, everything will work out fine. I love Mark DeVries's comparison of this approach to youth ministry with gambling. "The leaders of the church cross their fingers and believe, with all their hearts, that *this time* the cards will fall in their favor. This time, they'll find the superstar youth director who will change everything . . . fast."[3] They don't want a youth pastor; they want a *messiah*—someone with the charisma and competence to attract kids, keep them coming and make disciples out of them.

In a humbling parade of youth ministry shame, we keep watching kids walk out the back door of the church and away from their faith. Maybe it's time to shed the messiah complex that seems to come with the call to youth ministry and recognize that if we want to look back on our youth ministry years with any degree of satisfaction, we'll need to figure out how to access the incredible number of assets that parents bring to the table.

First, *parents love their kids more than anyone else*. This truth alone gives parents a tremendous advantage in the influence department. I'll be perfectly honest here. As a youth worker, I have never loved a member of my youth group—ever!—like I have loved (and still love) my own kids. There really is no substitute for the incredible depth and breadth of parental love.

Of course, we don't have to go too far to find parents who don't seem to love their kids—who over-discipline them, verbally or physically abuse them or fail to give them the time and nurture they need. Bad examples of parental love abound. But the vast majority of parents do love their children even when they don't know how to express it very well.

Again, that's why God's love is often described as the kind of love a father has for his children. There is no greater love. The apostle Paul also compared his ministry with the loving relationship that a child has with his mother and father (1 Thessalonians 2:7-12). Parents have the potential to become a powerful illustration of God's love. The more we can help parents to love their kids well, the better your kids will understand the nature of God's love. The two are indelibly linked.

Second, *parents care about their kids more than anyone else.* I've always claimed to care about teenagers, but I know that I don't care about the kids in my youth group like a parent cares. I'm ashamed to say that over the years I've let more than a few kids slip through the cracks of my youth ministry. I just didn't do a very good job of including them or making them feel welcome. I may have forgotten their names (more than once) or never bothered to learn them in the first place.

Parents don't let their kids slip through the cracks. Parents have a vested interest in their kids that no one else has. They want their kids to succeed, to get good grades, to be the most popular kid in the school, to get the most attention in the youth group. If you've ever coached a little-league team, you know how hard it is to deal with parents who all think their kids should be in the starting lineup. Parents find it hard to be objective because they care so much. But this is a strength of parenting, not a weakness.

Third, *parents have more time with their kids than anyone else.* How much time do you spend with the kids in your youth group? Some of us are better at this than others, but even the most dedicated youth workers I know only spend an hour or two with kids each week compared with several hours per day that parents do. Do the math yourself. There's no way we can possibly compete with parents for time with teenagers, nor should we.

You've probably heard by now that there's no difference between "quality time" and "quantity time." You really can't separate the two or have one without the other. The only way you can get quality time is to have quantity time. In a youth ministry, we're lucky if the kids in our youth groups ever have one or two "quality" moments with us all year long. Try it sometime. Ask former students to name some really memorable moments in their youth group experience and they'll probably be a bit embarrassed that they can't think of too many. But ask them to name some meaningful times they have had with their parents and they'll give you plenty because they've likely had lots of time with their parents for them to take place.

Fourth, *parents have more authority over their kids than anyone else*. While it's true that children and teens are free moral agents who can decide for themselves what they believe or don't believe, their freedom to do everything else is pretty much limited by their parents. This is especially true for younger teens. Can they go to summer camp? Can they join the worship band? Can they lead a small group? Can they go on a mission trip? In most cases, parents are the people who ultimately make those decisions because they are usually the same people who write the checks.

I've heard many youth workers complain when parents don't allow their kids to participate in certain activities, or withhold youth group attendance as a means of disciplining their teenager. I agree that there are times when parents don't make the best decisions regarding discipline. But parents are the only ones who can make those decisions and we need to respect their decisions and help them to make good ones. Only parents can provide the discipline and boundaries that teenagers need.

BOND BREAKERS

When I first started working with kids in the 1960s, I think I knew that parents were important, but parents were not really my concern. I just assumed that Christian parents were more than likely going to be there for their kids and hopefully be a positive influence on them. I didn't worry too much about church kids in the youth group because they were already getting plenty of spiritual input and guidance from their parents.

My job as a youth worker (as I understood it at least) was to attract non-Christian kids and lead them to Christ. That's what I did in Youth for Christ and that's what I assumed my role in the church would be as well. The church was weak in the area of youth outreach and evangelism, and that was my specialty. I was a kid magnet. My job was to turn that small youth group into a large one, and that's exactly what I did.

Since then the role of the church youth pastor has changed and assumptions have been reversed. As youth workers, we no longer assume that Christian parents are spiritually training their kids. Instead, parents assume that *we* are doing it for them. And as youth culture has become much more aggressive and all-encompassing, there are few people, including parents, who intuitively believe that parents have the most influence on their kids. Most people these days assume that peers and the media trump a parent's influence every time. Even when parents consent to the idea that they might be the primary spiritual influences in their kids' lives, they still want the church to do it for them because that's what they are paying the youth minister to do.

One of the first books I ever read on this subject was Merton Strommen's *Five Cries of Parents*. The book was based on research that was done by his organization, Search Institute, in 1984 with some eight thousand adolescents and their parents. It was this book that really got me thinking seriously about parents and youth ministry in the first place. One of the things that Strommen pointed out in his book is that teenagers look first to their parents for guidance and direction and routinely follow in the footsteps of their parents "*unless the bond between the parent and teen has been broken or vastly diminished.*"[4]

This has formed the basis of much of my teaching on the influence of parents for many years, both at youth ministry conferences and at Understanding Your Teenager seminars. It has been reinforced by every major study on the topic of teen influences since. In summary, what I believe and still teach is that parents remain the primary influencers of their children all through their teen years *so long as they stay connected with their kids and remain involved in their lives.* Of course, there are many other influences on teenagers today—both good and bad—such as other significant adults (teachers, coaches, youth pastors), peers and the entertainment media, but they never outweigh the influence of parents.

But when the bond between the parent and teen has been broken or vastly diminished, as Strommen puts it, then the influence of parents also becomes broken and vastly diminished, allowing those other influences—even those that are harmful—to become the most powerful influences by default.

It's easy to see therefore why we need to encourage parents to keep that bond of influence strong by staying connected with their kids and exploiting the natural advantage they have to influence their kids and lead them to follow Jesus. It's also easy to see how youth workers sometimes like to assume the role of the hero by stepping into the gap that is created when the bond of influence is broken by the parents themselves. We all know parents who are unwilling to accept responsibility for the spiritual upbringing of their children, or are too busy to do it, or are hindered by brokenness in the family.

But as I've thought more about this over the years, the more I've come to realize that parents are not always the culprits here. Maybe youth ministry itself is part of the problem. Maybe *we* are the ones breaking the bond between parents and teenagers. Rather than divorce, death, work, busyness, abandonment, lack of concern and other forms of neglect on the part of parents being the bond breakers, maybe it's us.

Here's what I mean. Many parents today view the youth ministry as the place where they can drop off their kids and get them spiritually trained by professional youth workers who are being paid to do exactly that. The very existence of youth ministry has given parents a good reason for not being the spiritual trainers of their own children. What I'm saying is that if parents are abdicating their God-given responsibility to spiritually train up their kids because they think youth workers in the church should be doing it for them, then youth ministry is undermining a parent's rightful place as the primary influencer of their kids. Maybe *we* are the bond breakers.

UNDERSTANDING YOUR TEENAGER

In my early days of youth ministry I loved being the hero. But as I said earlier, all that changed when my own kids became teenagers. I realize now that what I want my kids to gain from their youth ministry experience is exactly what the parents of kids I've worked with for years have wanted. They don't want a youth pastor with a messiah complex, they want their kids to follow and serve the true Messiah. We now know that the best way to make that happen is to help parents pass their faith on to their own children.

Once I started connecting all the dots on this issue back in the 1980s, I decided to do something about it. The first thing I did was to start paying a lot more attention to my own kids. And I also started paying a lot more attention to people who knew something about raising teenagers. The more I read and the more I listened to those who had a lot more experience and wisdom than me, the more convinced I became that youth ministry needed some resources for helping parents.

We weren't sure exactly what to do at the time, so we did what we were familiar with—we created an event. Our National

Resource Seminar for Youth Workers had been successful so we decided to create a seminar for parents using the same model. We rounded up the best team of experts on parenting we could find and put together a seminar for parents to help them become better parents. Since "the cry for understanding" was the first of Strommen's "five cries of parents," we chose the name Understanding Your Teenager for our seminar. We tested it in several locations, making adjustments in both the content and the seminar format, and then rolled out our first UYT seminar tour in 1988. All of our presenters were veteran youth workers who had raised teenagers of their own. While our attendance numbers were disappointing, the seminar itself got nothing but rave reviews.

When the YS executive team made the decision to cut our Understanding Your Teenager seminars because they weren't making money, I was extremely frustrated, because they weren't about making money; they were about helping youth workers reach out to parents with a resource that could impact the lives of kids in ways we could never do ourselves. I had become convinced that youth ministry of the future was going to include parent ministry in some way.

Not wanting the seminars to die completely, I kept our team of seminar presenters together, and my wife Marci booked a few seminars for us out of our home. At Youth Specialties, we went ahead with a video curriculum called *Understanding Your Teenager,* featuring Ken Davis, a friend from our YFC days. He had some great comedy routines about raising teenagers, so I played the straight man, and we ended up with a pretty effective resource that remained in the YS catalog for ten years or so.

When I left Youth Specialties in 1994, the only thing I took with me was Understanding Your Teenager. To me it represented the future of youth ministry, a trend that I wanted badly to reinforce and fan into flame if I could. My goal was not only to come alongside parents with training and resources but to encourage youth workers and other youth ministry organizations to do the same. I started writing books for parents, expanded our team of Understanding Your Teenager presenters, hired some office staff and began scheduling hundreds of seminars.

While we were out racking up frequent flier miles and speaking to half empty rooms of parents in church basements all over the United States and Canada, a pioneering youth pastor in Tennessee caught a similar, smarter vision for helping parents and articulated it beautifully in a classic book titled *Family-Based Youth Ministry*.[5] Mark DeVries not only gave a name to the movement but influenced an entire generation of youth workers to think about youth ministry in an entirely new way. You can't really do youth ministry without taking parents into consideration, he suggested. Family-based youth ministry isn't a program but rather a paradigm shift.[6]

He was right, of course, and there are few youth workers today who wouldn't agree that effective youth ministry has to include the intentional engagement of parents and families.[7] Understanding Your Teenager, meanwhile, is alive and well, having merged with another ministry to parents, HomeWord, led by my friend and colleague Jim Burns.[8] From the Faith at Home movement to Think Orange there are many voices today calling youth workers and the entire church to better equip and encourage parents so that they can take advantage of their role as the primary spiritual influencers of their children. Any reinvention of youth ministry must include a ministry to and with parents.

2

GROWING UP NAZARENE
Thinking About Adolescence

What I really wanted to become was an architect.

That's because I loved to draw, and my father was a building contractor. He was grooming me for the construction industry, and since I had some aptitude in art, he often encouraged me to consider becoming an architect. I honed my craft by doodling in church during Sunday morning sermons, and rather than scolding me, my father just provided me with more paper.

By the time I was in high school, I was drawing floor plans for room additions and homes my father would build all over Ventura County, which at the time was an undeveloped coastal region some fifty miles north of Los Angeles. Some of those houses are still standing today.

The year I graduated from high school, I won a county-wide architectural plan-drawing contest sponsored by the local building contractors association. Along with a trophy, I received a little scholarship money and a part-time job at Fisher & Wilde, a leading architectural firm in Ventura. I was seventeen years old when I enrolled in Ventura Community College, majoring in architectural engineering.

Youth ministry was certainly never on my radar early in life.

I don't think it was on anybody's list of possible occupations in the 1950s and 1960s. After all, the word *teenager* had only recently been coined as part of the English language, and *adolescence* was at best regarded as a transitional stage—something most people grew out of pretty quickly. In those days, it would have been highly unusual for anyone to build a career on something as fleeting and faddish as youth ministry.

So how did I end up in youth ministry? Actually I don't think I ever chose youth ministry as a career. It chose me.

GROWING UP NAZARENE

I grew up in a family that was very much like the families I watched on our black-and-white TV as a child, like *Leave It to Beaver* and *Ozzie and Harriet.* Dad went to work every day and mom stayed home to cook and take care of the kids. She was a *housewife,* which didn't sound at all politically incorrect back then. We were like all the other families in our community, except maybe for the fact that we were extremely religious.

Oh, there were lots of other religious families in those days, but we were over the top. We went to church twice on Sunday and at least once during the middle of the week. We didn't smoke, drink, dance, cuss, go to movies or work on Sundays. My parents were second- or third-generation members of the Church of the Nazarene, and they helped start two new churches—one in Oxnard, California, and another a few miles away in Camarillo, where we moved when I was in the sixth grade. We not only got saved, we got *sanctified.*

Since there were no junior high schools in our school district, I went to a public K-8 school. Vivid memories of my rather difficult seventh- and eighth-grade years have always provided a strong foundation for my work over the past forty years with junior high students. When you've been beaten up by the school bully three or four times or *pantsed* in front of a room full of giggling junior high girls, you find it pretty easy to empathize with kids who are trying to learn some social survival skills, find a few friends, figure out what kind of person they want to become and (if they are Christian) how to avoid being treated like someone with a contagious disease.

That was me in junior high school and I'm fortunate that I had help and encouragement from an eighth-grade teacher named Colgate Clark. For some reason, Mr. Clark liked me, listened to me and got on my case when I messed up. Sometimes he would offer to drive me home from school, and I can still recall many of the conversations we had in his car. Times (and teachers) have definitely changed since then.[1]

I was the oldest of four kids. Once I was old enough to swing a hammer, I went to work for my dad doing carpentry, painting and other construction jobs. We spent quite a lot of time together in his shop or on job sites where we would work side by side nailing down roofs, putting up sheet rock, hanging doors. By the time I was in the ninth grade, I could frame a house pretty much by myself.

I'll never forget the Christmas I opened a crudely wrapped gift from my dad. It was a genuine leather nail pouch with several loops and pockets for hammers, tape measures and other construction tools. I knew right then that he was sending me a message. I was now one of his *men*. Not long after that, he put me on the payroll at two dollars an hour—a lot of money in those days.

SUNDAY SCHOOL AND NYPS

My first personal experience with anything resembling church youth ministry was the Sunday school class I attended as a junior higher. Our teacher's name was Laura Baughman, a supersized woman with an even bigger heart. Her son Danny was in the class, but she loved all of us like we were her kids too. We had some memorable class social activities at her home where she would teach us all how to bake cookies and pull taffy. She also taught us a lot about the love of Jesus, mainly by example.

My high school Sunday school teacher was an energetic young man named Jerry Riddle. He was our pastor's younger brother and one of the funniest guys I've ever known—always cracking jokes or doing amazing things like turning his eyelids wrong-side out. I can't tell you how many times I have caught myself repeating something I heard Jerry say or doing something I saw Jerry do. He had a big influence on me.

Jerry was probably the first person I ever knew who did youth ministry pretty much the way we do it today. He took us out for sodas after the evening service, planned beach parties and organized miniature golf tournaments. He'd call us up after school to see if we wanted to hang out or go shoot some hoops. Sometimes he'd call just to see how we were doing. Jerry never went to a youth ministry seminar or read a book explaining why he should do these things. He just did them because he cared about us and wanted to spend time with us.

Interestingly enough, my parents weren't all that fond of Jerry. He had a habit of planning activities that interfered with my chores and other responsibilities around the house. I think they felt he was somehow in competition with them for my time and allegiance. Later on when I became a youth pastor myself, I reminded myself of that when scheduling activities for my youth group.

Besides Sunday school, we Nazarenes had the NYPS (Nazarene Young People's Society) which I began attending when I turned twelve years old. When you turned twelve in our church, you became one of the *young people*. I remember how our pastor would speak of teenagers that way—as young people. "It's so good to have the *young people* here on the front row," or "The *young people* will be having an ice cream social on Saturday night." The word *teenager* still had a subversive or rebellious sound to it and wasn't quite acceptable as part of a Christian's vocabulary—at least not a Nazarene's. But we young people would refer to ourselves as teenagers anyway, knowing full well that we were being quite worldly and risking the very salvation of our souls.

Our NYPS met on Sunday nights before the evening service in the fellowship hall. It was much like other denominational youth organizations that were in vogue around that time: the Walther League (Lutheran), the Epworth League (Methodist), the Westminster League (Presbyterian), and so on. They were all patterned somewhat after the International Society of Christian Endeavor, a youth organization which still exists today.

Our NYPS meetings were more or less informal versions of our regular church services. Rather than singing hymns from the hymnbook, we sang gospel choruses like "Gone Gone Gone Gone, Yes My Sins Are Gone," "Christ for Me" and everybody's favorite, "The Hash Chorus":

> Every day with Jesus, I'll be walking down the
>   King's Highway.
> Tell me the old, old story,
> I love him better every day, Hallelujah!
> I will make you fishers of men,
> If you'll only follow me.
> Hallelujah, what a Savior!
> I'm from sin set,
> You're from sin set,
> We're all from sin set free!

That was the contemporary Christian music of its day, and we loved it.

Our NYPS meetings also included lots of announcements and usually a Bible lesson involving students in some way with an object lesson or some kind of skit. I went to NYPS faithfully during most of my teen years, as did my parents. That may sound odd but my early recollection of our NYPS was that even though it was for the youth, it also included lots of adults, even seniors. Our church may not have been typical but our "young people's society" served as a something of a bridge between childhood and adulthood for the youth of our congregation, a way for them to get involved in the life of the church.

But I was a typical teenager of that period. You might even say I was one of the first class of teenagers, since some think the word was practically invented about the time I became one.[2] The baby boom generation was just beginning to emerge and the entertainment industry in particular was gearing up to take advantage of it. I was captivated by all the new music that was being created especially for teenagers. Elvis Presley, Frankie Avalon, Ricky Nelson, Buddy Holly, the Shirelles, the Everly Brothers and the Beach Boys provided the soundtrack for my generation. We were the first generation to have television in our homes and it was becoming a lot more interesting, with new shows like *Gunsmoke, Bonanza, The Twilight Zone* and *Candid Camera*. One of my personal favorites was an afternoon show featuring a goofy, slightly risqué comedian named Soupy Sales. When I was in high school, my friends and I would rush home from school to watch the latest episode. I memorized most of his routines and can still do a pretty good Soupy Sales impression to this day. I'm sure my parents were worried sick that Soupy Sales was leading me down the path to ruin.

I think about adolescence now a lot more than I ever did

when I was actually experiencing it. My memory of my adolescence is not particularly vivid, no doubt the result of repression, our normal tendency to forget the unpleasantness of the past. Adolescence for most of us was a time of life characterized by crises and catastrophes, one after another, which explains why so many people have such a hard time remembering what it was like to be a teenager. For most of us, it's a forgettable time of life. At training events I often lead youth workers and parents through a few exercises just to jog their memories a bit.

But when I was a kid, adolescence was quite a bit different than it is today. For one thing, it didn't take up half your life. For most of us, it was a half-dozen years or so spent going to junior high and high school, then it was time to get on with your life and do something important like get a college education, a job, a spouse or join the military. By the time we were eighteen years old, most of my generation was ready to get out of the house and start living lives of our own. I've attended a few of my high school reunions over the years and for the vast majority of my classmates that's exactly what we did (not always with success, but at least we tried).

Today the number of teenagers who feel prepared, let alone willing, to take on the mantle of adulthood at age eighteen is practically nil. There's a growing consensus that adolescence now extends well into one's twenties and early thirties. A few years ago *Time* magazine featured a cover story on a new demographic group called the "twixters," young people between the ages of eighteen to twenty-five who find themselves stalled in a "strange, transitional never-never land between adolescence and adulthood, putting off the iron cage of responsibility that constantly threatens to come crashing down on them." According to *Time*, on average young people say that adulthood begins at around age twenty-six.[3] Many have no idea at all when they become adults.

THINKING ABOUT ADOLESCENCE

Most of us have a pretty clear understanding of what it means to be a child or what it means to be an adult, but the definition of adolescence is not so clear. I have often defined it as one's transition from childhood to adulthood. Others equate adolescence with the changes that take place in a child's life which are associated with puberty. Some say it's a separate stage of life which can be further divided into more substages: early adolescence, middle adolescence and late adolescence. Still others say it's just a state of mind that represents a juvenile or immature way of thinking.

I've argued for years that adolescence is an artificial category—a way of categorizing, stereotyping and infantilizing teenagers which has in my opinion done them much more harm than good. This is an issue which gets debated quite a bit in youth ministry circles these days and for good reason. We have a vested interest in adolescence as a stage of life. If there were no adolescence there would be no youth ministry. It's safe to say that the invention of adolescence led to the invention of youth ministry.

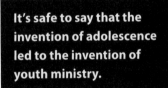

It's safe to say that the invention of adolescence led to the invention of youth ministry.

Most historians agree on when adolescence was invented. Credit is usually given to the famed developmental psychologist G. Stanley Hall, who first wrote about adolescence as a stage of life in 1904. In his massive (1,373 pages) volume *Adolescence: Its Psychology and Its Relations to Physiology, Anthropology, Sociology, Sex, Crime, Religion and Education*, he set in stone a theory about young people which continues to be pretty much universally accepted today. According to Hall, adolescence (the time of transition between childhood and adulthood) is a tumultuous and chaotic period of *storm and stress* for young people, a time of "savagery," with its "tribal, predatory, hunting, fishing, roving, idle, playing proclivities."[4]

I may not have vivid memories of my teen years, but I'm pretty sure my adolescence didn't include too much savagery—except maybe for the hunting and fishing part. When I was about twelve years old my dad gave me a .22 rifle which I frequently used to shoot gophers right out of their holes in our back yard. And I still like to fish, so I guess some of us never grow up.

Hall's famous description of adolescence as an inevitable time of turmoil and rebellion has led to many changes in how we treat teenagers in America. It has changed how we educate them, how we employ them, how we govern them, how we raise them. Some research suggests that teens today are subjected to more than ten times as many laws and restrictions as are most adults. If they weren't prone to rebellion before we enacted all those laws, they certainly are now. You would rebel too if there were special laws to keep you in line.

Researcher Christian Smith comments about the widespread and persistent negative stereotype about American teenagers:

> In U.S. culture, the very ideas of "teenager" and "rebellion" are virtually synonymous. . . . But that impression is fundamentally wrong. What we learned by interviewing hundreds of different kinds of teenagers all around the country is that the vast majority of American teenagers are exceedingly conventional in their religious identity and practices. Very few are restless, alienated or rebellious; rather, the majority of U.S. teenagers seem basically content to follow the faith of their families with little questioning.[5]

There are many who believe what has been called the "myth

of the teenage werewolf,"[6] a terrible picture of adolescence which says that as soon as puberty strikes, children inevitably turn into uncontrollable monsters who wreak havoc on their homes, families and communities. Some parents hold to this myth, thus allowing it to become a self-fulfilling prophecy. Kids generally live up or down to how they are treated, as most people do. If someone is treated as immature and imbecilic, they will probably end up acting that way.

We haven't always treated young people this way. As Paul wrote to young Timothy, "Don't let anyone look down on you because you are young" (1 Timothy 4:12). We have a treasure trove of biblical heroes to inspire teenagers who want to do something significant with their lives for God: Moses, Joseph, Samuel, Esther, David, even Jesus himself, who at age twelve declared "I must be about my father's business." King Josiah began his successful thirty-one-year reign in Jerusalem when he was eight years old. Joan of Arc was only nineteen when she was martyred for her faith. There are many examples in history of teenagers who showed remarkable competence and courage as they assumed roles that today are reserved more or less exclusively for adults. And young people today are just as capable, if not more so.

In this morning's newspaper I read about Zac Sunderland, a seventeen-year-old who lives not far from where I grew up, in Ventura California. He became the youngest person in history to sail around the world alone. His voyage spanned three oceans and five seas, and twice led him across the equator. He went sixty hours without sleeping while trying to fix broken rigging in fifteen-foot seas and gale-force winds. He even encountered a band of pirates. He endured brutally long windless periods while bobbing cork-like beneath a blazing sun, eating canned food and drinking nothing but tepid, desalinated water. Arriving at his home port, he told reporters,

> I think society puts young people in a box—people 15, 16,
> 17—and doesn't expect them to do much but go to high
> school and play football and stuff like that. This just shows
> they can do a lot more with some strong ambition and
> desire. My [advice] is to get out there and do your thing
> with all you got.[7]

Dr. Robert Epstein argues in his book *The Case Against Adolescence: Rediscovering the Adult in Every Teen* that most of the negative behaviors we see in teenagers are not the inevitable result of being adolescent but rather the unintended consequences of the artificial extension of childhood well past puberty.

> Through most of human history, our ancestors began to
> produce children shortly after puberty, just as the members of all nonhuman species do to this day. Whether we
> like the idea or not, our young ancestors must have been
> capable of providing for their offspring, defending their
> families from predators, cooperating with others, and in
> most other respects functioning fully as adults. If they
> couldn't function as adults, their young could not have
> survived, which would have meant the swift demise of the
> human race. The fact that we're still here suggests that
> most young people are probably far more capable than we
> think they are. Somewhere along the line, we lost sight
> of—and buried—the potential of our teens.[8]

For years I've taught parents and youth workers to think about adolescence differently. I don't deny that adolescence exists, but I don't think of it as a separate stage of life that is fundamentally different from childhood and adulthood. Rather I view adolescence as a transition between the two which is gradual and progressive. As Bruce Narramore titled one of his books many years ago, *adolescence is not an illness.*[9] Not only is it not an illness, it doesn't even need a cure.

I've always enjoyed working with middle-schoolers, because they are quite often in the eye of the storm, so to speak. Every day they become a little more adult, a little less child. The middle school group at my church grows (literally) six inches in one year. Every year when we graduate our eighth graders out of the middle school group, the whole group gets short again.

The space between childhood and adulthood is actually a blend of the two. The goal of adolescence is to not be one any longer than you have to. Why remain in a transitional stage for the rest of your life? But many people are doing this with regularity today. When we treat teenagers as if they are neither children nor adults, we tend to isolate them. The "space between" then become a chasm from which teenagers see no hope of ever leaving.

I have met many adults who have no point of reference from which to relate to teenagers. Not being teenagers themselves, they don't feel comfortable around adolescents. How different this would be if they viewed them instead as young men and young women who were aspiring and preparing to become adults much like themselves. Then the mentoring could take place that every teenager needs.

> The goal of adolescence is to not be one any longer than you have to. Why remain in a transitional stage for the rest of your life?

I've always loved the apostle Paul's description of his own transition from childhood to adulthood. "When I was a child, I talked like a child, I thought like a child, I reasoned like a child.

But when I became a man, I put childish ways behind me" (1 Corinthians 13:11). This was likely a reference to his *bar mitzvah* at age thirteen when he was swiftly ushered into adulthood in a ceremony that was familiar to all Jewish families. Following his induction into adulthood, he was no longer thought of by his family or community as a child, but rather as a young man who was capable of making good choices, contributing to the family and taking on more responsibilities. Of course this didn't happen overnight. Young Paul needed guidance and direction from his parents and mentors as well as opportunities for on-the-job training. But everyone reading Paul's letter to the Corinthians would certainly have understood the illustration and have easily applied it to the point he was trying to make. "As a child learns when he becomes a man, so shall we someday understand."[10]

We don't have rites of passage like that anymore. Families and communities don't spend their entire lives in small villages. Not too many people grow up on farms (unless you're a farmer's kid) nor do they attend one-room schoolhouses out in the country. The world has become a much more complicated place than it was a hundred years ago or even fifty years ago when I became a teenager. But none of that changes the fact that children still—sooner or later—grow up to become adults. Whether it's sooner or later is something we have more control over than most of us realize. Adolescence until age thirty and beyond is not inevitable.

I know this is true because I have seen what happens when parents choose otherwise. I don't always admit this publicly, but I am a big fan of bluegrass music. Since my college days I have been seriously involved with bluegrass and have had the opportunity to hang out with many of the incredible musicians who make this unique kind of music. Bluegrass music may not be everyone's cup of tea, but nobody argues with me when I say that bluegrass musicians are some of the most talented in the world.

Most people regard bluegrass as an older genre of music—played by old timers like those on TV shows like *Hee Haw* and *The Beverly Hillbillies*. But surprisingly there are many young bluegrass musicians taking up the music every year—turning out hit records that rival anything being made by older generations of musicians. I have paid special attention over the years to these young professional bluegrass musicians. I'm always fascinated by them. I often wonder what made them decide to adopt the alternative lifestyle of a bluegrass musician over the music and lifestyle which is being so heavily marketed to teenagers today.

One of the most popular young bands in bluegrass right now is a group called Cherryholmes, a family band made up of a mom and dad plus their four kids. In 1998 when Jerry and Sandy Cherryholmes lost their oldest daughter to health problems associated with teen drug abuse, they made a decision to protect their other children from the same fate. They moved the family from their Los Angeles home to a farm house in northern Arizona, as far from the city and the drug culture as they could get. They began homeschooling their kids and learning to play musical instruments—guitar, mandolin, fiddle, banjo, bass. None of them had ever played bluegrass (or any kind of music) previously, but they made it a family goal to play together as a band at a few bluegrass music festivals. In less than two years, they had not only accomplished that but much more. I won't give you their entire amazing history here, but I've had a chance to spend time with these very talented, articulate and mature young people, and I'm always reminded that it's still possible for today's teenagers to comfortably and competently take their place alongside adults if and when they are given the chance to do so.

I could tell you many other stories of parents like these who made the decision to raise their children differently from how the world says it should be done. I know that it's not possible for all parents to homeschool their children or move to the desert. But I do believe that it's possible for us to start treating teenagers in our churches differently from how the world typically does. Rather than assuming that teenagers can't handle adult sermons or adult music or adult conversations, they should be invited to participate fully in the life of the church. We have done our youth a great disservice by segregating them from the adult population of the church and giving them only "milk" when they are capable of so much more. Robert Epstein comments about the infantilizing of teenagers:

> What happens when you treat a whole segment of the population as if it's inferior and helpless? As blacks and women can tell you, many people in such a sub-population tend to believe what they're told and then to behave as expected. . . . But as blacks and women have demonstrated over the last century, performance can be a very poor predictor of competence. When we infantilize teens, we might create many of them in the image we have in mind, but that doesn't necessarily tell us about their potential.[11]

I sometimes hear from parents who express concerns that the very elements of adolescent culture they are trying to steer their kids away from are actually being used to attract teenagers to the church youth group. I know parents are often misinformed and have a tendency to overreact to a lot of the programming we do in youth ministry, but in recent years I've found myself sympathizing with these parents more often than not. I have always believed in communicating with teenagers in a language they can understand, but there comes a time when we need to stop treating them like children and more like the young men and women they are. Our goal in youth ministry is to help our kids grow toward maturity in Christ Jesus. The image of the youth ministry as the "toy department of the church" needs to change.

When I conduct Understanding Your Teenager seminars, I always remind parents that despite what they've heard to the contrary, their goal is to work themselves out of a job. Hopefully by the time their children leave their teen years, they will have the skills and capabilities they need to survive on their own.

I still have the leather nail apron my dad gave me so many years ago. I'll always be grateful to him for it. I don't think he ever meant it to be a rite of passage, but his gift certainly symbolized his high regard for me and his expectations of me. And while I can't say that I lived up to all of my father's expectations of me, I know I didn't live down to G. Stanley Hall's.

TEENS TELLING TEENS

I attended church regularly as a teenager and participated in just about everything my parents did. I realize I probably didn't have much choice in the matter, but I don't remember ever refusing to go to church. I had lots of friends there (including my girlfriend who was also the pastor's daughter) and I wanted to at least give the appearance of being a good Christian. Not going to church in those days was considered one of the seventeen or so deadly sins and I didn't want to have the whole church thinking I had *backslidden*. I sometimes tell people that I stayed out of trouble as a teenager largely because I had too many people to disappoint. That's very true when I think of the church I grew up in.

But as the 1960s rolled around and teen culture became more of a force to be reckoned with, some of the teenagers in my church were getting restless and bored. Our little Nazarene church didn't have a youth ministry nor did it have any intention of starting one anytime soon. While we didn't have a youth group, I was involved with the NYPS, sang in the adult choir and helped teach children in the Sunday school from time to time. Still, I remember questioning much of what I had been taught as a child. Our church was very legalistic and I couldn't understand why God had such a big problem with things like going to movies and dancing. I never rebelled against my faith or strayed too far from it as a teenager, but I really can't say whether or not I would have remained on that path for the rest of my life were it not for a fortunate turn of events in our family.

Youth for Christ (YFC) was one of several nondenominational parachurch youth ministries that were still gaining in popularity in the 1960s. While the Young Life movement was spreading fast in some parts of the country, Youth for Christ was the dominant youth ministry in Southern California, with successful franchises in San Diego, San Bernardino, Los Angeles, Fresno, Santa Barbara, Long Beach and Ventura County, where I lived.

Known for the large youth rallies that were held on alternating Saturday nights, YFC also sponsored clubs which met on local high school campuses with the motto "Teens Telling Teens." The evangelism strategy behind those clubs was for teenagers to invite their friends to either their local YFC clubs or to the Saturday night rallies where they could hear a gospel message, usually presented by a popular youth speaker.

Toward the end of my junior year in high school, my father was invited by a business acquaintance of his to join the board of directors for Ventura County Youth for Christ. We weren't familiar with YFC at the time because Nazarenes generally didn't associate with non-Nazarenes. The YFC rallies in Ventura were held either in a Foursquare church or a Baptist church, and quite frankly we weren't sure people who went to churches like that were actually going to be in heaven with us. But my dad broke the rules of Nazarenedom and enthusiastically joined the board of YFC. When he found out there was a YFC club at Camarillo High School where I was a student, he strongly suggested I attend.

Dad rarely encouraged me to participate in extracurricular activities like clubs or sports because they interfered with my work for him and other responsibilities around the house. But he wanted me to go to YFC club. I looked into it and found out that Camarillo High's club met every Tuesday afternoon in a yellow smoke-belching church bus with *Jesus Is the Way the Truth and the Life* printed in big letters on the side of it. Every Tuesday afternoon that old bus would pull up in front of the school right after classes were over and start honking its horn. There was no way I was going to get on that bus in full view of my friends at school. But my dad kept urging me to go, so I finally relented and got up the courage to sneak aboard that church bus, hoping that none of my friends would notice.

I was surprised to discover that not all of the students who attended YFC were the losers I thought they were. One of the best players on our high school basketball team turned out to be the president of the club. The club director was a big guy with a wide grin whose name was Sam McCreery. I liked him and thought he was *very* cool.

I started attending YFC club pretty regularly and decided that it wasn't so bad after all. I got more involved and began attending the twice-monthly Saturday night rallies, which brought together members of all the YFC clubs in Ventura

County. These rallies were unlike anything I had ever experienced at church, with a wide variety of singers, actors, athletes, magicians, ventriloquists and every other kind of Christian entertainer you could imagine. There was also spirited competition between schools in a crazy kind of Bible quiz program featuring uniformed participants who had memorized entire books of the Bible. They would take their places on the stage while the quizmaster read off questions in a careful and dramatic way. Chairs were rigged with electronic seat pads to identify who stood up first, giving that person the right to correctly answer the question. Sometimes these Bible quizzers were off their seats before the question was even asked. This was all very impressive and completely new to me.

As part of the "Teens Telling Teens" strategy, YFC clubs in those days usually involved students in leadership roles. At the beginning of my senior year of high school, I was elected president of Camarillo High's YFC club. I'm pretty sure it's because I was one of the only boys in the club. (Remember, this was 1962.) After getting elected president I helped plan our club meetings, which were now meeting at a church near the school rather than on the bus. The club had grown; we were averaging around thirty students at our weekly meetings.

It was customary at YFC's year-end meeting to ask attendees to fill out a small registration card with their name, address and phone number, and then to turn it in after the meeting was over. That card was also used to register decisions to receive Christ at the end of the meeting in a discreet sort of way. Any student who wanted to make a decision was invited to simply tear off the corner of the card before they turned it in. This would save anyone the embarrassment of raising a hand or coming forward during an invitation hymn. After the card was turned in, the YFC club director would follow up if a student indicated that he or she had made a decision. I discovered that one of my presidential responsibilities was to speak at that last meeting of the school year.

About seventy-five kids showed up that day to watch me break into to my very first flop sweat. I gave a talk on Ecclesiastes 11:9 (I still have it memorized) with what felt like a mouth full of cotton. I was petrified and probably awful, but something important happened to me that day. *Three students* tore off the corner of their cards. It both amazed and thrilled me. Quite honestly, I was hooked. From that day forward I knew what I wanted to do with the rest of my life.

As a youth worker, I love giving teenagers opportunities like that. There's no doubt in my mind that today's young people are just as capable as those of my generation to assume the mantle of adult responsibility and hear the call of God on their lives. When we stop infantilizing them and treating them as mere consumers of youth ministry entertainment, they just might grow out of adolescence—which is absolutely necessary to become mature adult followers of Jesus Christ.

MY FIRST YOUTH MINISTRY JOB

Thinking About the Message

My call to youth ministry came in the form of an actual phone call.

After I graduated from high school in 1963, I went to work for the architectural firm that gave me a job after I won the drafting contest. After several weeks working for the architectural firm I was absolutely bored to death. On top of that, I noticed how bored (and boring) everyone else there seemed to be. I wasn't so sure I wanted to become an architect after all.

A few weeks later Don Goehner, the executive director of Ventura County Youth for Christ, called me and wanted to know if I'd be interested in working part time for YFC as a club director. My responsibilities would include running one of the high school clubs, helping out with Saturday night rallies and doing some graphic design work. He also wanted me to help start a new junior high club program. The pay would be fifty dollars a month.

I was stunned and absolutely overjoyed. It took me all of five seconds to say yes to Don. I definitely wanted that job. The pay didn't matter. I was only seventeen years old, and gas was only thirty-five cents a gallon. What mattered was that I got to do something I really wanted to do, what I believed God was calling me to do.

I finished up the summer working at the architectural firm and began my career in youth ministry in September 1963. I became a part-time YFC staff as well as a full-time college student. Still majoring in architectural engineering, my courses seemed irrelevant. I breezed through a five-unit calculus and analytic geometry course, but I had no idea how I was going to use that in my work at YFC. Still I managed to complete a year of studies with decent grades.

But when it came time to sign up for my sophomore year of college, I decided to change my major. I still remember the blank, puzzled look on the face of my college counselor.

"Tell me again what career you're considering?" she asked.

"Youth ministry," I answered.

"Hmmm . . ." she said as she flipped through her college counseling manuals looking for the mysterious career I had just identified so that she could recommend a new major or a few courses that would apply. Youth ministry wasn't listed anywhere, so apparently the career didn't exist. She finally suggested that I major in sociology or psychology, since I would then be able to study adolescent development, family systems and the like. So that's what I did.

I was a sociology major for a semester or two but came to the conclusion that it just wasn't practical enough for me, so changed my major again to speech and drama, reasoning that a lot of youth ministry involved putting on skits and giving talks. I took several classes that had me memorizing lines from Shakespearean plays, learning how to apply realistic makeup and competing on a debate team arguing the pros and cons of the Vietnam war. It wasn't exactly what I had in mind.

I changed my major again and finally graduated (after seven

years of college) with a degree in graphic design, which turned out to come in very handy later on when we started Youth Specialties. God does lead you down a crazy path sometimes to get you where he wants you to go.

CAMPUS LIFE

I learned a lot about youth ministry during my first year at YFC, most of it by trial and error. I also learned a lot about Youth for Christ. Even though the organization was only as old as I was, it had a rich history. Past and present YFC leaders like Billy Graham, Torrey Johnson, Jack Wyrtzen, Ted Engstrom and Jack Hamilton were legendary. YFC's national headquarters were in Wheaton, Illinois, which I discovered was something of an evangelical holy land. There were hundreds of local "rallies" spread out all across America and around the world, with literally thousands of YFC clubs meeting every week. Some rallies owned their own auditoriums and even had radio and television stations. YFC had its own monthly magazine and sponsored a huge conference every summer in Winona Lake, Indiana, which drew thousands of teenagers to a national talent competition and Bible quizzing championship. The more I learned about YFC, the more impressed I was and proud to be part of it.

Not long after I joined the staff of Ventura YFC, we attended a regional staff training retreat that was held at Palomar Baptist Camp in the mountains near San Diego. YFC's new national club director, Jay Kesler, was going to be there, as well as other staff from Wheaton and all over California. I was excited about getting to meet all these people and learning more about what was going on in other YFC programs.

I don't remember the exact date of the retreat, but I know it was winter because when I arrived at the camp, there was about a foot of snow on the ground. As I walked down a slippery path leading into the main conference room, I surprisingly got whacked in the back of the head with an icy-hard ball of snow. I heard someone yell, "Nice shot, Mike!"

That was my first encounter with Mike Yaconelli. A club director at San Diego YFC, he was pretty well known as one of the most popular speakers for YFC rallies all over the state. He had been the speaker at a couple of Ventura YFC rallies when I was a senior in high school, and I remember being very impressed with him. He made me laugh and seemed to be the epitome of cool with his rock star hairdo and Italian swagger. Getting hit in the head with a snowball by Mike Yaconelli seemed to me a special way to get welcomed to this retreat.

In 1963, things were changing in YFC, and changing fast. One of YFC's ministry's mottos was "Anchored to the Rock, Geared to the Times" which meant that while the *message* would never change, the *methods* were always up for grabs. That was certainly true in the mid-1960s. The old YFC club which had already become a sacred cow to many was rapidly being discarded in favor of the hipper, more outreach-oriented Campus Life club. We learned all about Campus Life there on Palomar Mountain.

Campus Life originated in San Diego—the brainchild of Ken Overstreet, Jim Green and Mike Yaconelli—and it involved more than just a name change. It was a complete overhaul of the club program with a new emphasis on reaching "pagan" kids. While YFC clubs certainly had an evangelistic purpose, they tended to attract far more Christian kids than non-Christian kids. Like the club I attended at Camarillo High School, YFC club was something of an oasis for church kids who were comfortable singing lively choruses and hearing gospel messages. Very few non-Christian kids attended YFC clubs for the simple reason that they were too religious. It was also hard to get YFC Clubs onto high school campuses for the same reason.

Campus Life clubs, on the other hand, didn't *sound* religious and they didn't *look* religious. They were programmed entirely for nonchurched kids. I was amazed when I heard the numbers being reported. Most of the Campus Life clubs in San Diego were *averaging* three hundred kids per club. Some had more than five hundred kids showing up every week. Hundreds of teenagers were making decisions for Christ. These were staggering numbers compared to what we were used to in Ventura.

How did they get results like those? We learned that the first rule of thumb was to stop meeting in churches. Kids didn't want to go to a church in the middle of the week. So in San Diego, all the clubs were either held on campus in the gymnasium or auditorium, or in neutral locations like community centers, shopping malls or homes. Apparently there were some big houses in San Diego.

Second, we learned that Campus Life had to be promoted effectively. The magic was in the marketing. No longer could you depend solely on Christian kids to invite their non-Christian friends (the idea behind YFC's teen-to-teen philosophy). Instead, Campus Life required mass-market advertising to create interest and name recognition among the general teen population. This was called *image-building* and it included an elaborate publicity campaign utilizing posters, stickers, flyers, handouts and unusual publicity stunts like the "tub pack."

I'm not sure who came up with the idea for a tub pack, but it was in all likelihood an adaptation of the popular phone-booth packing competitions that were all the rage on college campuses at the time. Schools competed with each other to see who could stuff the most students inside a phone booth and still get the door closed.

The tub pack was based on the same concept. A brightly painted bathtub was mounted on a trailer and pulled from school to school, usually during the lunch hour. The Campus Life director would then get on a bullhorn and challenge students to "break the world's record" for how many kids they could get inside (or on top of) the tub. The only rule was that no one who was in or on the tub could touch the ground. With *Campus Life* prominently stenciled on the side of the tub, this was a strange but very effective attention-grabber which sometimes made the local TV news (hopefully not because someone had suffocated on the bottom of the pile).

Third, Campus Life club meetings had to appeal to a non-Christian audience. Jim Rayburn, the founder of Young Life, is well known for saying "It's a sin to bore a kid,"[1] but YFC in San Diego definitely took that concept to new heights. Campus Life clubs were anything but boring. They started at 7:17 p.m. ("An Unusual Time for an Unusual Program") and featured a steady stream of crowd breakers, games, skits and crazy stunts—like the famous (or infamous) "electric chair" or "hot seat," a wooden stool outfitted with a six-volt battery and a model-T Ford engine coil. The stool was wired to give the person sitting on it a mild electric shock that sent them flying off the seat to the applause and laughter of the audience. The electric chair was demonstrated at our Palomar Mountain retreat, and of course everybody wanted to know how to build one.

Campus Life meetings weren't all fun and games, however. Everything led up to a "clear presentation of the gospel." But rather than students giving testimonies or a speaker presenting a gospel message, the Campus Life strategy was for the director to lead a discussion on a relevant topic like sex, drugs or the war in Vietnam. "Rap sessions" were in vogue at that time, so discussion topics were promoted in order to attract kids who had opinions on that topic or just wanted to hear more about it. The discussion was primarily a set-up for the Campus Life director who would skillfully slip a short gospel message into his "wrap up" and then invite kids who wanted to know more to stick around during the refreshment time.

The electric chair notwithstanding, the big idea behind Campus Life was to provide a nonthreatening environment that would attract non-Christian kids and keep them hanging around long enough to hear the gospel. In some ways, the Campus Life philosophy was an early incarnation of what is today being used by thousands of seeker-sensitive churches, which ditch the trappings of religious language and traditions and rebrand themselves with catchy names. But in 1963 it was all very new and exciting to me, and when our staff returned to Ventura we had a whole new game plan. We adopted the entire Campus Life program and tried to copy almost everything that had worked in San Diego, albeit on a smaller scale. San Diego for example had put on a city-wide "Hippo Hunt," a kind of treasure hunt involving busloads of kids following clues all over town to find the secret location of a live hippopotamus. We had no idea where to find a hippo, so we used a goose from our back yard (we raised them) and had a "Wild Goose Chase" instead.

As our club program in Ventura morphed into Campus Life, so our Saturday night rally program also began to change. While the basic pattern of wholesome Christian entertainment plus an evangelistic message stayed the same, rallies became less frequent (from bimonthly to monthly) and more in tune with the pop culture of the day. If you listened to the radio, you could hear a new musical trend. Doo-wop and Motown were fading in popularity and folk music was becoming very cool. Artists like Bob Dylan, Joan Baez, the Kingston Trio and the New Christy Minstrels were topping the charts and appearing on network TV shows. Coffee houses with live folk music were packed with young people and folk festivals attracted thousands more to hear the strumming of twelve-string guitars and banjos and to sing along.

It didn't take long for us to figure out what to do at Ventura YFC. We started calling our Saturday night rallies "Hootenanny!"[2] replacing our past parade of gospel quartets and trumpet trios with folk groups. I took up the banjo and learned to play well enough to form a folk trio with one of our guitar-playing club directors and my fiancée Marci West, who played the upright bass. A cross between the Smothers Brothers and Peter, Paul and Mary, we told corny jokes and performed songs like "Tie Me Kangaroo Down Sport" and "If I Had a Hammer," truly cutting edge stuff back in those days.

After Marci and I married, we formed a bluegrass group with my brothers Jim and Joe, called The Rice Kryspies. My brothers were still in high school at the time and they learned to play guitar and mandolin while I continued to work on my banjo playing. With Marci on the bass, we were busy almost every weekend performing at YFC rallies, camps and churches all over Southern California. There were very few Christian folk groups in those days, so we stayed busy and recorded a couple of albums which we sold to kids for $5 each. We actually sold quite a few of those old LPs and they turn up from time to time on eBay.

We went to great lengths coming up with new and creative ways to present the gospel to kids. Music became my primary means of communication, but I know other YFC staff who learned stand-up comedy, acting, magic and ventriloquism just so they would have a few more tricks of the trade at their disposal for keeping kids' attention. All of us worked hard to become better speakers. Back in those days we needed to be able to present a captivating three-point gospel message with the skill and flair of an infomercial pitchman.

For as long as I can remember, youth ministry has always been about finding ways to attract the attention of teenagers so that the message of the gospel could be presented. YFC's goal was to reach unchurched teens with the good news about Jesus. While Young Life chose relationships over showy events as a strategy, the goal was still the same—to share Christ effectively with teenagers. They just took a more soft-sell approach. Other parachurch youth ministries like Campus Crusade and Inter-Varsity Christian Fellowship were also evangelistic or missional in nature, utilizing strategies appropriate for the audiences they were trying to reach.

But the gospel always remained central to the mission. As Paul wrote, "We proclaim him, admonishing and teaching everyone with all wisdom, so that we may present everyone perfect in Christ" (Colossians 1:28).

THINKING ABOUT THE MESSAGE

When I was in seminary, I took a class in comparative theology from one of my favorite professors, Dr. Bernard Ramm. One of his assignments was to write an essay answering the question "What makes a church different from a meeting of the local Rotary Club?" At first this seemed to me like a very strange question, and I wasn't really sure how to answer it. Who cares what the difference is between a church and the Rotary Club? But the more I thought about it, the more important the question became to me.

The answer, of course, is Jesus. When all is said and done, when you take away everything that both Rotary Clubs and churches have in common—meetings, membership, traditions, liturgies, social activities, belief in a higher power, teachings on living a morally upright life, service projects and all the rest—the only thing that sets the church apart from any other humanitarian organization is Jesus Christ and what he accomplished for us on the cross.

This difference makes all the difference in the world. To quote Paul again, "For what I received I passed on to you as of first importance: that Christ died for our sins according the Scriptures, that he was buried, that he was raised on the third day according to the Scriptures" (1 Corinthians 15:3-4).

I've thought about that question of Dr. Ramm's a lot over the years in regards to youth ministry. When it's all said and done—when you take away all the meetings and worship bands and burger bashes and camps—the bottom line is always what Paul identified as "of first importance." Are teenagers leaving our youth groups secure in the knowledge that Jesus died on the cross for their sins and has provided for them not only eternal life but a whole new way of living their lives right now?

According to some of the research that has been done lately on the spiritual lives of teenagers, it doesn't appear that young people are getting that message. According to researcher Christian Smith, what many teenagers are leaving our youth groups with is a new kind of American religion, which he calls "Moralistic Therapeutic Deism." The basic creed of this religion goes something like this:

1. A God exists who created and orders the world and watches over human life on earth.

2. God wants people to be good, nice and fair to each other, as taught in the Bible and most world religions.

3. The central goal of life is to be happy and to feel good about oneself.

4. God does not need to be particularly involved in one's life

except when God is needed to resolve a problem.

5. Good people go to heaven when they die.[3]

Smith interviewed hundreds of teenagers, many who were raised in churches with youth ministries, and he found that when they talked about their faith, they didn't talk about being forgiven for their sins, putting their faith and trust in Jesus, accepting the free gift of salvation made possible by the finished work of Christ on the cross, celebrating the Lord's Supper, worshiping God with their families and with the church, praying or reading the Bible or any other uniquely Christian practice. Instead, as Smith puts it, "the dominant religion among U.S. teenagers is centrally about feeling good, happy, secure, at peace. It's about attaining subjective well-being, being able to resolve problems and getting along amiably with other people."[4]

Michael Spencer, a former youth pastor and blogger, wrote a thought-provoking piece about youth ministry which appeared in a recent issue of the *Christian Science Monitor*:

> We evangelicals have failed to pass on to our young people an orthodox form of faith that can take root and survive the secular onslaught. Ironically, the billions of dollars we've spent on youth ministers, Christian music, publishing and media has produced a culture of young Christians who know next to nothing about their own faith except how they feel about it.[5]

Strong words. How did this happen? I don't think there are too many youth pastors who are teaching Moralistic Therapeutic Deism to the teenagers in their youth groups. Most youth workers I know would say they have been doing their best to teach the gospel week after week. That our youth are not getting the message is not necessarily because they haven't heard it or aren't being taught it. But perhaps we're sending other messages to teenagers that are just coming across a lot louder and clearer than the message we want them to hear. The wholesale conversion of our teenagers to a religion like MTD may be nothing more than the unintended result of a systemic weakness in how we pass faith on to the next generation.

THE GOSPEL OF COOL

One of the hallmarks of evangelical youth ministry for as long as I've been involved is that we have done everything possible to make Christianity as appealing to young people as we could. That's one of the things that attracted me to YFC when I was in high school. Like most teenagers, I wanted to be cool. Unfortunately, the church I attended wasn't very cool. I would have never invited one of my friends from school to go with me to church. Truth is I was embarrassed by my faith when I was at school or with friends. We Nazarenes didn't do all the things that other people seemed to do just to have a good time. I always felt like I was part of a cult.

But YFC was cool. And as youth culture changed in the mid-1960s, YFC went from cool to groovy. Campus Life's image-building campaigns utilized many of the images of psychedelia and the summer of love. We staged huge city-wide events like "Happening '68" which featured an elaborate stage set patterned after the popular TV show *Rowan and Martin's Laugh In* ("Sock it to me!"). We put together musical acts to mimic popular artists like the Mamas and the Papas and the Beach Boys. I'll never forget the night when several of us on the YFC staff dressed up like the Beatles and sang "I Want to Hold My Nose" (about a girl who was body-odor-challenged). From the response of the screaming crowd, I think some of those kids thought we actually *were* the Beatles. Each week we tried to incorporate as many culturally relevant elements into our programming as we possibly could so that teenagers could plainly see that they didn't have to give up their coolness to be a Christian.

This has been a primary communication strategy for effective youth ministry for decades now. We've moved from cool to groovy to rad to excellent to awesome to . . . hot, all for the purpose of reaching teenagers for Christ.

Music been a huge part of this strategy because it has served as a common language for teenagers. It wasn't long after Larry Norman burst on the scene in the early 1970s as a kind of evangelical Mick Jagger that an entire Christian music industry emerged to give youth workers in the church easy access to thousands of artists and entertainers who could help bridge the gap between a two-thousand-year-old story and the ever changing musical tastes of teenagers. The problem today, of course, is that there is no longer a common language, musical or otherwise. The Christian music industry has become a tower of Babel.

I'm reminded of this every time I'm in a youth worship service with a room full of teenagers who are trying to decide whether or not they like the music that's being played up on the stage by a group of musicians who aren't really very good but earnestly doing their best to sound like the David Crowder band. I look around the room, and quite honestly I'm not sure I would see a worse example of enthusiasm for worship if these kids were being asked to sing Gregorian chants.

I'm not criticizing contemporary worship music. I'm just wondering if we don't sometimes allow the medium to become the message, as Marshall McLuhan once put it. Have we blurred the distinction between what we have to do to look and sound cool and what we need to do to help students come to know Jesus personally, to become firmly grounded in their faith and learn to worship God with sincere hearts?

There's nothing wrong with cool, but sometimes the message of the gospel simply gets lost in it. I have heard of an ancient Jewish tradition in which a rabbi would put honey on the Torah and allow children to lick it off, thereby associating God's Word with sweetness. I've always loved that idea, but I have worried about what happens when the children lose their appetite for sweetness and want something with more substance. There has always been a danger with connecting the gospel with the bells and whistles of youth ministry. Truth is, the gospel is not always going to look or sound very cool, and our kids shouldn't be conditioned to believe otherwise.

THE GOSPEL OF SIMPLE

When I was in YFC, there was always a mandate to make a *clear presentation of the gospel* at all of our events. This forced us to simplify things quite a bit, because we didn't have much time. In most cases, kids were there for just a few minutes and then they were gone. Some of them we would never see again. So we had to be clear and quick. It was always a challenge to get everything we needed to say into a ten- or fifteen-minute talk and then ask kids to make a decision based on the information you had just given them.

Curiously we often do the same thing in the church, as if we're afraid we won't see our students again the following week. We trim things down so that after all the fun and games and "worship" at least our students can leave with a little bit of truth, the point of the day. I know that many youth ministries provide programs for core students who want to go deeper in their walk with Christ but because this is the less visible part of the program it often suffers from lack of resources, personnel and attention. It's really no wonder so many young people are hard pressed to explain anything at all about what they believe.

In Christian Smith's words, Christian teenagers are "stunningly inarticulate" concerning the content of their faith.[6]

I remember when Bill Bright, the founder of Campus Crusade for Christ, simplified the gospel in a little booklet called *The Four Spiritual Laws*, which was first published in 1965. Being a former businessman and evangelist, he condensed the plan of salvation into a handy list of bullet points which, if nothing else, were clear and concise. At YFC, we bought those little four-law booklets by the case.

Over the years we've had a similar tendency to want to simplify our faith so that kids can remember it and pass it on to others. From "One Way" (1970s—raise a finger) to "God Rules" (1980s—raise a fist) to "What Would Jesus Do?" (1990s—wear a bracelet) to "Love God, Love Others" (2000s—wear a T-shirt or get a tattoo), every generation has its own version of the gospel made into a slogan of some kind.

There's nothing wrong with keeping things simple, of course. Moses reduced the faith of the Israelites to a couple of lines that could easily be passed from one generation to the next (Deuteronomy 6:4-5). But he also gave parents clear instructions on how and when to teach those lines to their children on a daily basis. And in Hebrew tradition, the children were taught to ask "Why?" and "What does this mean?" so that parents could tell the stories of faith to their children and explain why their God was so different from all other gods.

Every generation of Christians needs to be taught the core stories and doctrines of the faith from the Word of God. They can't be sloganeered or reduced to a bumper sticker. It has been said that the Christian faith is only one generation away from extinction and in many respects that is true. Unless parents and other caring adults take time to instruct the next generation in the faith, there is no guarantee that the faith will continue. Without a solid biblical foundation, the Christian faith can easily morph into Moralistic Therapeutic Deism or some other form of popular religion.

It would seem that the church understood this better in the days before youth ministry. Confirmation classes for young people often consisted of two years of rigorous training in the doctrines of the faith. The Mormons still get it. They require their teenagers to spend several years in "seminary" and then to serve as a missionary learning their faith while having to explain it to others, often at great personal cost and humiliation. It should come as no surprise that Christian Smith's research found Mormon young people to be far more confident and clear about what they believe than youth from evangelical churches.[7]

But we live in an age of the simple. From text messages to Twitter, we really don't have time for a lot of depth. With so much information to digest these days, most people are content to know that the information they want is available somewhere, whenever its needed. Students today often say that they don't need to study history or learn to do complicated calculations in mathematics because they can now access all of that information on the Internet or utilize computers to do the same tasks in a fraction of the time. It's there on a need-to-know basis. Likewise for many young people, it's enough know that God is there if he's needed. Meanwhile they have more important things to do with their time.

THE GOSPEL OF WOW
Everyone knows that today's postmodern culture emphasizes experience over reason, familiarity over facts. You can know only what you know; that is, you can only trust what you've experienced for yourself. In a postmodern world, authority

comes at a great discount and personal experience is valued over everything else. As youth ministry has embraced the postmodern worldview, many youth workers have turned almost exclusively to the gospel of wow to lead young people to Christ. If we can just give kids a "wow" experience, then they'll come to understand and know the truth of the gospel.

The gospel of wow is not really new, of course. When the Jesus Movement was in its heyday we assured young people that they could get high on Jesus, an alternative to grass and acid which of course would provide them with the ultimate wow experience. Over the years we've used mission trips, small groups, learning games, simulations, role plays, camps and retreats, contemporary worship experiences and anything else we could find that would move kids from passive to active involvement in the learning process. All of these things can be beneficial, of course, but they become dangerous when truth is sacrificed for technique.

Having been in the idea business for a long time, I know that youth workers tend to shy away from topics that are boring or not easily illustrated or *experienced* by teenagers in some way. I have to confess that I have been guilty of gravitating to the gospel of wow. Like many youth workers, I'm always on the lookout for new illustrations (I've written several books full of them), object lessons, PowerPoint slides, video clips, anything that will grab the attention of kids so that they will have a "wow" experience. I can't tell you how many times I've used what I thought was a very effective illustration in a youth talk only to discover later that the kids had no idea what I was trying to communicate. But they do remember (even liked!) the illustration.

We make the assumption that young people just don't process information like generations of the past did (and therefore most of the adult population). Because they are postmoderns, they prefer everything in sound bites, rapid-fire images, personal encounters and digital downloads. There's some truth to all that, but I still believe that young people can handle good preaching and teaching. Despite rumors to the contrary, teenagers will still listen to people who have something to say and who treat them respectfully and avoid talking down to them. Of course youth should be encouraged to attend the regular worship services of the church where good preaching is (hopefully) happening all the time. Youth pastors might try out their preaching skills on the entire church congregation from time to time. If it won't fly there, it probably won't fly with the kids either.

The Bible says to preach the word "in season and out of season" (2 Timothy 4:2). I take that to mean even when it's not the popular or trendy thing to do. I don't do a lot of speaking to groups of teenagers (I don't get many invitations to do so) but when I do, I find them to be much more responsive than many adult groups. Kids don't hate preaching. They just hate boring, badly prepared sermons like we all do. Sometimes we think that because we are speaking to teenagers, we don't have to prepare like we would if we were preaching to adults.[8] But teenagers are not stupid; they can recognize bad preaching for what it is. They just don't want us to waste their time with a lot of empty words. If we are truly communicating the life-changing, radical, revolutionary Word of God to kids, they can become energized and transformed by it just as generations before them.

THE GOSPEL OF ME

Closely related to the gospel of wow is the gospel of me. In his insightful book *Christless Christianity*, theologian Michael Horton comments on the biblical illiteracy of many of today's young people and also on the gospel of me:

It does not really matter any longer whether one has been raised in an evangelical family and church—understanding the basic plot of the biblical drama and its lead character is as unlikely for churched as for unchurched young people. God and Jesus are still important, but more as part of the supporting cast in our own show.[9]

Horton is making reference here to one of the main themes of Moralistic Therapeutic Deism which gives *me* and my preferences the place of first importance. My story becomes the central plot of God's story. As journalist Jeff Jarvis writes in his book *What Would Google Do?* the essential rule of the new age is "Give the people control (and we will use it)."[10] Young people today are unwilling to cede control of their lives to anyone else unless they have no other choice. That's just how the world works now.

The gospel *is* of course about ceding control over our lives to someone else, which is why it's such a hard sell these days. But the liberating news of the gospel is that we don't have to be in control, we don't have to live the perfect life, we don't have fix all the world's problems or "be Jesus" to the world. We can give our lives in obedience and out of love for Christ and follow him as one of his disciples.

I visited a church recently which promoted itself in the community with the slogan "Make it *your* church" reminiscent of the old burger jingle "Have it *your* way." Years ago we used that slogan as an example of what a self-centered society we were becoming, but now we've just adopted it for the purpose of connecting with emerging generations who believe that *I should be able to have everything the way I want it.* I should be able to choose the church that I like, the people I want to fellowship with, the music that I sing, the sermons that I listen to, the parts of the

Christian faith that I like or want to believe. Do we really have to sell the gospel this way? I would think that it would be good news to young people to know that they don't have to create their own religion or find their own way to God. That has already been done for them by the only one who is really capable of doing it. That's what makes the gospel such good news.

On occasion I like going into a good restaurant and not always having it "my way." I'd like the chef to just prepare the best meal he can make and deliver it to my table—his or her way. Just bring it on. That's a little bit what the gospel is like. The Christian faith doesn't present us with a menu selection from which we can choose our own spiritual path. Instead it invites us to a banquet which has already been prepared for us and is now ready to eat.

SPIRITUAL DISCIPLINES

In 1989, Mike Yaconelli and I (and our wives) spent a week with Henri Nouwen at his home at L'Arche Daybreak in Richmond Hill, outside of Toronto, Canada. Overall, it was a significant experience for all of us. Henri coached us through a daily regimen of prayers and spiritual practices which helped me realize that it truly is possible to feel intimate with God. Nothing magical or mysterious happened there, but Henri gave us the tools and the encouragement and the time we needed to experience God in a very special way. I'll always be grateful for that.

No matter how hard I have tried, I have not been able to duplicate that week with Henri Nouwen at home. The spiritual breakthroughs that I experienced in Canada just don't seem to happen very often in Lakeside where I live. I know that God can show up anywhere and I'm familiar with the spiritual disciplines which lead to intimacy with God and I practice them with some regularity. But I have found that I just can't count on having amazing spiritual experiences whenever I want to have them. I fast, I pray, I read Scripture, I gaze at beautiful works of art and listen for the voice of God but more often than not he is silent.

But my faith and my confidence in God does not depend at all on how close I feel to him each day of the week. I learned many years ago that mountaintop experiences usually happen only on the mountain. They are wonderful when they do occur and they remind me that God still breaks through from time to time but I need something more than that to keep me firm in my faith.

I really appreciate the trend in some youth ministry circles toward a more Jesus-centered, reflective approach which encourages students to read Scripture, pray, fast and practice other spiritual disciplines.[11] All of these practices are beneficial and should flow naturally from our love for and devotion to Jesus. But I sometimes fear that putting these practices at the center of our youth ministries shifts the emphasis ever so slightly away from what Christ has done for us to what we do and what we experience.

Let me make a comparison to marriage. Marci and I have been married for forty-four years now, and I'm convinced that our marriage has remained strong because we are just as committed to marriage as we are to each other. In other words, the *fact* of our marriage has had just as much to do our staying together all these years as our feelings about each other at any given moment. Even when we don't like each other very much, we remember that we married on a particular date and made vows to each other that we both fully intend to keep until "death us do part."[12] While over the years we have had many wonderful romantic, tender and intimate moments together (and still do), the enduring and unshakable truth of our marriage is what keeps us together, no matter what.

The Christian faith is likewise based on a truth—the story of our salvation—which is fully capable of keeping us connected to God even when our personal experience with God falls short. The story of our redemption—of how Jesus Christ came and was crucified, buried and rose again on the third day—is the truth that our young people need to hear again and again. There are plenty of religions, self-help programs and party drugs that will provide them with intense spiritual experiences, but only one gospel will save them from their sins. Our young people need to be reminded constantly—as we all do—of that enduring and unshakable truth about a great price that was paid for us on the cross so that we could have intimacy with God every hour, every minute, even when we don't feel close to him at all.

There's nothing wrong with programs that attract teenagers. I still believe in putting honey on the Torah. We need to speak the language of young people, meet them on their own turf and communicate effectively. But having been in youth

> **Today's high-tech fest will be tomorrow's hootenanny.**

ministry now for more than forty-five years, I can assure you that youth ministry trends will continue to come and go. Today's high-tech fest will be tomorrow's hootenanny. Even the relationships that kids have with their youth leaders—as valuable and important as they are—will in all likelihood be temporary. The only thing that really matters, and certainly the only thing that will never change, is the truth of the gospel. If we aren't getting that right, we aren't doing very good youth ministry.

4

THE BIRTH OF YOUTH SPECIALTIES
Thinking About Programs

In the fall of 1965 I attended a weekend youth workers retreat sponsored by Forest Home Christian Conference Center, a camp in the San Bernardino Mountains. While Forest Home was well known as one of the top camping programs in the state, this was my first time there. Founded in 1938 by Henrietta Mears (also the founder of Gospel Light Publications), both Billy Graham and Bill Bright (of Campus Crusade for Christ) reportedly received their calls to ministry at Forest Home.

The Southern California Youth Workers Fellowship was organized in the mid-1960s by Jim Slevcove, the program director at Forest Home. It met once or twice a year for networking and idea sharing. Sometimes there would be a speaker and a few workshops on various topics. To my knowledge this was the first youth worker gathering of any kind in California and maybe the whole country. It brought together a select group of people who were working with kids in the church as well as in parachurch organizations like YFC and Young Life.

I was invited to lead two workshops, one of them on how to work with junior high kids. Our junior high program at Ventura YFC had picked up some momentum by this time and we were running several junior high after-school clubs, plus a monthly rally called "Junior High Jamboree." Hardly anyone in youth ministry worked with junior high kids in those days as junior high students were still considered children—too squirrelly and immature for "real" youth ministry. This was the first of many workshops that I would eventually lead on junior high ministry. My other workshop was on how to silk-screen posters, something I had learned to do my first year in college. Posters were the web sites of the 1960s. Every concert, every event, every movement had to have a poster, an eye-catching piece of artwork that attracted attention and gave the event some legitimacy. Psychedelic posters were especially popular, with their fluorescent colors and surrealistic designs. So we silk-screened psychedelic posters for Campus Life with snappy slogans like "Tune In, Turn On, Drop In . . . at Campus Life!" Everybody wanted to learn how to silk-screen, so I brought all my gear to the retreat and put on a little demonstration.

While there, Jim Slevcove asked if I would be interested in a summer job. He was looking for someone to run their junior high camps—a job held the past two summers by Mike Yaconelli. Mike's position at San Diego YFC had changed and he no longer had his summers free. Forest Home ran twelve weeks of junior high camp at what was then known as the Lost Creek Ranch.

I explained to Jim that I was getting married soon and that my wife would need a job too. Not a problem, he said, and so Marci and I joined the Forest Home staff at $100 a week for the two of us plus room and board. That didn't sound bad at all in those days. We were going to earn $1200 for twelve weeks of summer and have few if any living expenses. We actually managed to save most of our paychecks and felt a little bit rich.

Marci and I worked two summers at Forest Home and loved

every minute of it. Jim Slevcove also hired my brothers to work at Forest Home so that The Rice Kryspies could perform at camps during the summer. We worked two summers there with some incredibly gifted people and learned a lot about camping, junior high ministry and how to survive as a married couple under adverse living conditions. Today our son Nathan is the junior high director at Forest Home, now a year-round position.

After our first summer at Forest Home, Marci and I moved from Ventura to San Diego, where I took another part-time job as a Campus Life director. I hadn't planned to move to San Diego. In fact, in the spring of 1966 I was offered a part-time position on the staff of Fresno YFC, one of the most successful programs in the state. That's where I really wanted to go. I had become good friends with several of the staff in Fresno, and they had a folk group in need of a banjo player. I was ready to move north.

But sometime before I finalized my decision to take the Fresno job, I got a call from Mike Yaconelli suggesting that I visit San Diego and consider a move south. They had a position open for me if I was willing to come, and San Diego also had several four-year colleges where I could finish my education.

I knew it would be a great experience to work with the guys in San Diego. They were doing some amazing things with the Campus Life program there and I definitely wanted to be part of that. I couldn't believe they wanted me to come there.

Surprisingly my visit to San Diego wasn't convincing. It only confirmed my decision to move to Fresno. I was from a small town, and San Diego just seemed so . . . *big.* The ministry there also looked overwhelming to me and I wasn't sure I could pull off everything they wanted me to do. I wasn't sure I could handle the pressure.

So I declined San Diego's offer and drove home to Ventura, thinking I would call Fresno the next day and accept theirs. But on the four-hour drive home, I continued to pray about the decision, and by the time I got home I had changed my mind—or, more likely, God changed it. I have no other way to explain any of that except to say that God wanted me to move to San Diego. I've never forgotten that experience—how God sometimes calls you against your will. It took several years before I came to appreciate that God knew what he was doing.

I spent the next two years as a Campus Life director in San Diego. While my time there was fruitful, it was also very difficult. Like most everyone else, I was paid part-time and worked full time. YFC's executive director Ken Overstreet required maximum commitment and maximum ministry output from everyone who worked under him.

I'll never forget how stressful our mandatory weekly staff meetings became as each one of us had to report how many kids attended our club meetings, how many decisions were made, how many follow-up appointments were made, how much time we spent in the office, even how many hours we spent praying. I really grew to hate those staff meetings.

But I loved the ministry side of YFC. It was an incredible time to be involved with Campus Life which was still growing and having a huge impact in the San Diego area. Some of our events were drawing thousands of kids as we rode the crest of what came to be known as the Jesus Movement. Teenagers were coming to Christ hundreds at a time. I ran several Campus Life clubs, led the junior high program and did most of the graphic design work for YFC, all the while trying to finish my college education.

That wasn't going so well, however. In the fall of 1967, I flunked three of the four courses I was taking at San Diego

State—not because they were difficult, but because I never had time to attend class. My marriage wasn't doing too well either. Marci quit school to work full-time because my income from YFC just wasn't enough for us to live on. We rarely had time for each other. When she got home from work, I was off to another club meeting or YFC event.

In the spring of 1968 I drafted a letter of resignation and mailed it to Ken. It was an agonizingly difficult decision for me at the time because I loved YFC so much. YFC had given me my calling in life and almost all of my most important relationships, including my wife. Like my decision to leave Youth Specialties twenty-five years later, this one hurt badly.

After mailing the letter, I called Mike. He and I had become pretty close friends, and I knew he would sympathize and understand my situation. We were both married (unlike most of the YFC staff) and we were both having a tough time finishing school. Six years earlier, Mike had begun his college education at Bob Jones University in South Carolina and was famously kicked out because of his unwillingness to conform to the school's unusually strict codes of conduct. Now, just like me, he was trying to get his degree from SDSU, which seemed almost impossible while working for YFC. Mike was also getting a lot of pressure from his wife at that time to get a real job.

I told him what I had done. "I mailed a letter of resignation to Ken this morning. I need to finish school. I have no idea what I'll do next, but I know I can't keep on working for YFC."

"You can't quit," Mike said.

"Why not?"

"Because I just quit too."

When Mike and I decided to leave Youth for Christ, neither of us knew what we were going to do next. Our first order of business was to just finish school. I still had more than a year of college to go, assuming San Diego State would let me back in. Mike was in pretty much the same boat.

We also needed jobs, so we found a couple of churches willing to give us youth ministry positions. Since I had grown up in the Nazarene Church, I managed to get a part-time job as the youth director at San Diego First Church of the Nazarene. Mike found a position at a Southern Baptist church in the San Diego area and started working with kids there. Neither of those churches paid us much (about $200/month as I recall) so Mike continued to book himself out as a speaker. I still had my family folk group, The Rice Kryspies. We mailed out a brochure promoting ourselves around Southern California as a package deal for churches and camps—music by The Rice Kryspies and a message by Mike Yaconelli.

But we weren't entirely finished with YFC. San Diego's new Campus Life program was now being copied by YFC rallies (regions) all over the United States. While some areas of the country were slow to make the change, YFC's national leadership was committed to the new

Mike and the Rice Kryspies together

Campus Life program. Even the name of *Youth for Christ* magazine had changed to *Campus Life*.

The problem however, was that some YFC programs around

the country were changing the name of their clubs to Campus Life but still operating them just like their old YFC Clubs. In January 1968 at the annual YFC national staff conference called "Midwinter," Mike wrote and distributed a broadside titled "Campus Life Is Not Just a Name." In it he wrote:

> When we changed the name from YFC clubs to Campus Life, we were not just changing a name. We were changing a program. This program was designed to meet the needs of the high school segment of society today."
>
> There was a growing feeling that some of our clubs had become spiritual sanctums for social misfits—others, only excuses for Christian kids not to share their faith personally with their friends because they had made a poster, called a speaker, or just attended the club meeting, thus fulfilling their Christian responsibility to their schools.
>
> Some of us, as directors, were frustrated because we never knew when we went to a YFC club meeting whether the publicity would be effective and we would be speaking to non-Christians, or whether it would just be the same old crowd and we would be giving them a Christian challenge (usually a good kick on the back of the lap) and hope that the next week things would be different!
>
> Most of us can remember standing in the back of a room filled with kids—watching, as one of our club officers ruined the meeting because he was not prepared, or just couldn't hack it. We remember the animosity caused by club officers who were not dependable and the whole meeting would fall apart because of the officers failed to take their responsibilities seriously—but we couldn't replace them, they were board members' or pastors' kids! We had to stand by and watch some kid tube our whole pro-

gram—all in the name of "leadership development!"

Our greatest concern came with the realization that we were not really reaching very many nonchurched teenagers on the high school campus, nor were we effectively motivating our Christian kids through teen-to-teen philosophy—but we had a club, and we had meetings! Some of these meetings were the finest club meetings possible, but most were merely meetings. However many of us strongly felt that we were not in this ministry simply to organize meetings. We had a job to do, a ministry to perform—that of reaching the high school student where he was!

It has been only three short years since we faced these facts squarely. Those of us who had been club men can recall that it was not easy to drop the [old programs] in favor of the Electric Chair and other effective crowd breakers.

Another change was a definite move to a more director-centered program, eliminating much of the "officer problem" and insuring a consistent program by competent leaders. Many YFC club programs completely dropped elected officers feeling that it was more important to impress Christian teens with the fact that their foremost responsibility was to invite a non-Christian to Campus Life.

Our [Campus Life] program continues to change and develop. Many of these changes are apparent even to the casual observer. However, it is obvious that there are still those in our YFC family who are frustrated by the old problems because they changed the name of their club program from YFC to Campus Life in an attempt to reach more kids—but they failed to change their program![1]

To help remedy this problem, Youth for Christ's national office decided to publish a manual for YFC staff around the country outlining the philosophy of Campus Life and providing all the ideas that made the program successful. Even though Mike and I had turned in our resignations, we were both enlisted by YFC to become part of the writing team to create the first YFC "Impact" manual.[2] Mike had already written several articles on the philosophy of Campus Life and had compiled hundreds of skits, crowd breakers, games, discussion starters and the like that we used in Campus Life, so he was an obvious choice for this project. My job was primarily to provide the artwork that was used to promote Campus Life. In San Diego I created most of the art that we used for handouts, posters and flyers, as well as the Campus Life logo, which was used for quite a few years.

So early in the summer of 1968 with briefcases stuffed with file folders, Mike and I flew to YFC's headquarters in Wheaton where we worked on the inaugural Campus Life "Impact" manual along with several other Campus Life staff from around the country. The project was completed in just a few days, and upon returning home, we turned in our keys to the YFC office in San Diego and were officially finished with Youth for Christ.

As might be expected from two ex-YFC guys, our youth groups closely resembled Campus Life clubs. We took all the experience we had gained in YFC and applied it directly to our youth groups. At First Nazarene, we had a weekly outreach meeting called "Sunday Night at Six" which featured skits, crowd breakers, discussions—just like a Campus Life club. Mike's youth group at Lemon Grove First Baptist was pretty much the same.

So we were anxious for the "Impact" manual to get published. Even though we knew what was in it, we wanted the convenience of having all those good ideas in one place—where they could be easily accessed. We knew they were going to be shipped out to YFC programs at the end of the summer and we were expecting to get copies as well.

Around the first week of September I got a call from Mike, who had gone by the YFC office to see if the manuals had arrived. "Well, I've got some good news and some bad news."

"Uh . . . what's the good news?"

"They're in. I saw one in Ken's office."

"And the bad news?"

"We can't have one. Only 'credentialed' Youth for Christ staff can have a copy of the new manual. We don't work for YFC anymore. We're not credentialed."

Needless to say, we were both pretty ticked off. Not only did we want to see the fruit of our labor, we also wanted the ideas that were printed in that book. While we had contributed much of the material that was in it, we knew it also included ideas that had come from other sources as well. We wanted to use those ideas with our church youth groups.

Despite our protests we never did get a copy of that first "Impact" manual. I remember being tempted to break into the YFC office and "borrow" a copy long enough to make copies but finally decided against that. What we decided to do instead gave us whole new careers.

THE BIRTH OF YOUTH SPECIALTIES

"Why don't we just write another one?" I suggested to Mike. "Let's create a manual full of the same kinds of ideas we put in the Campus Life manual—only this time we'll make them applicable to church youth groups. You do the writing and I'll do the layout."

It made perfect sense to both of us. We still had plenty of ideas in file folders. It would be easy enough to organize them once again into a book. If we published them ourselves, we could sell them cheaply to other church youth workers just like us. Maybe we could even make a few bucks.

So we set up a little workshop in the back bedroom of my apartment, where I had a drafting table, an IBM Selectric typewriter, a silkscreen and a few other art supplies. Mike brought over all his files and started typing. I worked on the design. Of course, we knew we couldn't publish a real book like the kind you bought at bookstores. Our plan was simply to get the individual pages printed at a local quick-print shop (these were brand new in 1968) on three-hole punched notebook paper and then put them into a notebook or folder of some kind. I could silkscreen something on the cover to make them look good.

We decided to call our book *Ideas* which Mike was fond of saying wasn't a very creative title, but it was definitely truthful—it told you what was in the book. No philosophy, just ideas. We did however include a paragraph on the opening page of the book labeled "Our Policy":

> We are dedicated to servicing the church. We believe that modern programming techniques open the way to new dimensions of youth ministry. Our aim is to provide functional creative techniques to both the experienced and inexperienced that they may create a youth program that is effective. Our purpose is to use programming as a means of communication that will reach an otherwise unreachable young person.

I don't remember whether it was Mike or me who wrote that paragraph, but it represented for us what would be called today a mission statement, maybe a manifesto. While we didn't spend a lot of time formulating our "policy," those few sentences pretty much summed up our approach to youth ministry and what we were trying to accomplish:

- First, we wanted to help churches do better youth ministry.

- Second, we believed that better programs lead to better youth ministry.

- Third, we believed that everyone should have access to good ideas.

- Fourth, we believed that the goal of youth ministry was to reach "unreachable" kids—those who found the church boring and irrelevant. That was what we did in Campus Life and that was what we thought church youth ministry should be doing as well.

After a day or two of typing furiously, we ended up with six chapters, including "Crowd Breakers and Stunts," "Games and Group Participation Stunts," "Publicity Ideas," "Special Events," "Contests, Prizes and Penalties," and "Skits." We had a lot more ideas in our files but decided fifty-four pages was a good place to stop.

As we were getting our book typed up and ready to print, we decided to give our little two-man publishing company a name. We weren't sure how YFC would respond to having these ideas broadcast all over the country so we wanted to protect our anonymity somewhat. It didn't take long for us to come up with a name. There was a store not far from where we lived, called Corvette Specialties, where you could buy parts for Chevy Corvettes and sometimes the cars themselves. Mike always dreamed of driving a Corvette and so he was well acquainted with the place.

"How about *Youth* Specialties?" Mike suggested. Honestly, I don't remember that we ever considered any other names. If we were starting a business today I'm sure we would do some market research, take phone surveys and conduct focus groups to make sure we had the perfect name. But Youth Specialties didn't sound too bad. So I quickly designed a logo—a rather stiff-

The original Youth
Specialties logo

looking square box with a YS reversed out of the center—and added it to our title page: "Copyright 1968 by Youth Specialties." Actually we had no idea what a copyright was or how to get one at that time, but it sounded important and looked good with our new logo.[3]

Next, we needed a mailing address. We tried to get a post office box but discovered we couldn't get one until we filed for a "fictitious name" with the city of San Diego. It took us a few days to figure out how to do that, but we got it done and Youth Specialties was in business—unofficially. It took us several more months to get a business license and do all the things businesses have to do to become legal in California.

I don't think it would be an exaggeration to say that we pooled our entire life savings (about $500 between us) to print up our first batch of *Ideas* books (about a hundred). Each of the fifty pages was single-sided and three-hole punched so that we could collate them and put them in notebooks. We used kids from our two youth groups to help assemble our books by strolling around two long tables in the fellowship hall at First Nazarene church and stacking the pages in neat piles. Then we inserted them into bright yellow report folders that I bought at the San Diego State bookstore upon which I had silkscreened in big red letters "Ideas" along with our snazzy new logo.

The first *Ideas* book

The only marketing plan we had at the time was to sell them for five bucks a piece at the Southern California Youth Workers Fellowship meeting at Forest Home. We wanted to gauge not only the sales potential of our book but also what the response from YFC would be.

It didn't take long to find out. While we sold all of our books at the retreat (sales potential: very good!), the you-know-what hit the fan (response from YFC: not so good). After the retreat, we began hearing from YFC staff not only from around Southern California but from all over the country. Our *Ideas* book became controversy number one. Some of our long-time friends in YFC were calling for our heads.

We were not to be deterred. We printed up more books and took them with us to the Greater Los Angeles Sunday School (GLASS) Convention, where we set up our first-ever Youth Specialties booth. I hand-painted a sign "Ideas for Youth Groups," which we taped across the front of our table in the exhibit hall. Again, we sold out of every book we had.

Feeling like we had probably exhausted the entire market for youth ministry books at those two events, we decided to write a second volume which we simply called *Ideas Number Two*. This one had a blue cover and contained another fifty-nine pages of crowd breakers, games, special events and skits, plus a new chapter called "Creative Communication" which included a few teaching ideas and discussion starters.

Many of the ideas that were published in those original *Ideas* books seem incredible today—not incredibly good but incredibly bad. It's hard to believe that we actually published in *Ideas Number Two* a collection of *put-downs*, a long list of insults that we recommended and encouraged youth workers to use on unruly or disruptive kids. A few examples:

- "The only reason we invited him tonight is to remind you

that every 60 seconds, mental illness strikes . . ."

- "You know, if Moses had ever run into this guy, there would have been an eleventh commandment!"

- "Her mouth is so big, she needs 20 minutes just to put on her lipstick!"

What could have possessed us to recommend such a mean-spirited list of slams? In the book itself, we explained that put-downs could be used to "(a) get laughs, (b) make your victim feel like a complete idiot, and (c) make *you* look like the big hero." Pretty embarrassing, I have to admit. All I can say now in our defense is that put-downs like these were widely used at Campus Life meetings (as well as in our youth groups) in the late sixties as a useful technique for keeping kids under control. They were considered an acceptable alternative to scolding or getting angry during a meeting, much like a stand-up comedian might use a witty one-liner in response to a heckler at a night club. We thought they were not only funny but rather humane. Of course we were wrong to use—let alone recommend—put-downs in youth ministry programming if for no other reason that they are stupidly counterproductive. Kids generally are unlikely to come back to a meeting when there's a risk of being humiliated in front of their friends. I don't remember when—but we eventually removed that list of put-downs from our *Ideas* books as well as dozens of other stunts and crowd breakers that victimized kids.

By early 1969, Mike and I had written and published three books. Also in a report folder format, *Ideas Number Three* had a brown cover with *Ideas* silkscreened down the front in yellow ink. It was the first of our books containing material contributed by other youth workers. One of the first contributors was Denny Rydberg, a friend of Mike's who lived in Anacortes, Washington, at the time. Denny sent in an idea called "Offering

Olympics" which made a competitive sport out of taking up the collection at a youth group meeting.

After *Ideas Number Three* was published, we decided to make a serious financial investment in Youth Specialties. Up to this point we had only sold our books at local events; now we wanted to try getting our books into the hands of youth workers all over the country. To do this we decided to place a full page ad in *Christianity Today,* which we discovered cost almost a thousand dollars.

It seemed like a long wait between the time I mailed the artwork for that ad and the time it was published. When the magazine finally came out, we were absolutely thrilled. There we were—Youth Specialties—looking very important in *Christianity Today.* We felt famous and just knew that everyone who saw

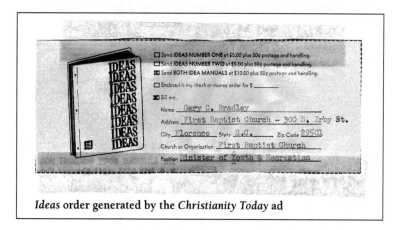

Ideas order generated by the *Christianity Today* ad

our ad would fill out the order form and mail it in to our P.O. Box with their $5 plus shipping and handling. We went to the post office every day expecting a deluge of orders. The deluge never came but we did get a trickle—three or four per day over several weeks. It was enough to eventually cover the cost of the ad and print more books.

Mike and I continued to work with our youth groups during the 1968-1969 school year while going to school and churning out our *Ideas* books. As we were collecting more ideas from other youth workers around the country, we decided to make *Ideas* a quarterly publication with yearly subscriptions. Youth workers could order the "next four volumes" for only $19.95.

We were growing weary of silk screening covers and collating stacks of paper, so by the end of 1969 when *Ideas Number Four* was in the works, we decided to get our new book printed at a real print shop and have them bound into real books. The advantages were obvious—our cost per book would go down and they would look a lot more professional. The disadvantage was that we would need to print larger quantities of books. We were used to printing around a hundred at a time. Now we would have to print several thousand at a time in order to make offset printing worthwhile. But we were starting to make more profit from our books (especially since we started selling books in advance with subscriptions), so we decided to go for it.

The first four books in the new format.

I redesigned the new book with an entirely new look and feel. We only printed on one side of each page which we explained by saying that the back side of each page was there for "note-taking." Truth is, we just didn't have enough material to fill up a whole perfect-bound book. We wanted each book to contain around two hundred ideas but when they were typeset, they got smaller. So to fill up space, we added pictures using our youth group kids as models. We published *Ideas Number Four* in this new format and republished our first three books the same way. Each book had a white cover with Ideas printed boldly across the front in a different color ink. They looked pretty snazzy when they were laid out on a table side by side.

Meanwhile, our relationship with YFC continued to deteriorate. All three of our books contained ideas that had been closely associated with Campus Life, and while a number of YFC leaders were sympathetic and supportive of what we were trying to do, many YFC staff considered us traitors. We were accused of ruining Campus Life's ministry by giving away their ideas to the church, to which we responded, "Then you're ministering to the wrong kids." Even though we may have been right on that one, our old YFC colleagues remained upset with us for years. Some of them thought YFC should bring a lawsuit against us for copyright violations, but back in those days nobody was able to figure out who stole what from whom, so no legal actions were ever pursued. Eventually most YFC staff decided to forgive and forget, as did we. In recent years Youth Specialties and YFC have even partnered to co-produce the national student event called DC/LA.

In my early days of youth ministry, I was an idea junkie—always on the lookout for a good idea for a new game, skit, crowd breaker, discussion starter, you name it. A good idea back then was like gold. Today, good ideas are a dime a dozen (free on the Internet), but in the sixties and seventies they were hot commodities, which is probably why YFC guarded theirs with such ferocity.

Why were ideas so valuable in those days? Probably because our identities as youth workers were so wrapped up in them. In both YFC and the church, my job as a youth director was to conjure up enough youth ministry bells and whistles to keep teenagers interested and coming back for more. That required lots of new ideas. You couldn't just keep doing the same thing over and over again.

THINKING ABOUT PROGRAMMING

In those days youth ministry was equated with programs. If you were a great programmer, you were a great youth worker. Programs had clear objectives, a beginning and an end. When it was over, you could stand back and admire your work. I loved creating incredible meetings. I loved getting up in front of groups of teenagers and being listened to and admired by young people. I admit it—I was a performer, an entertainer and in many ways still am. I need an outlet for that. And in my early days of youth ministry, my outlet was youth ministry.

Eventually I learned—after plenty of programming disasters—that youth ministry is not about me, nor is it about the success or failure of the programs I lead.

We were like drug dealers, Mike and I, pushing our ideas. Of course we had good intentions. We believed that youth workers ought to be able to find a good idea fast—whenever they needed one. We knew from experience that you could spend hours, even days, writing a skit or inventing a new game or crowd breaker, leaving precious little time to do the more important things in ministry. Our goal was to save youth workers time and eliminate the hard work of having to come up with new ideas.

During our first year in business, Mike and I were still trying to finish up college and working in churches part time. We ran Youth Specialties out of our spare bedroom for the first year or so. I cut and paste our *Ideas* books, flyers and other publicity materials back when "cut and paste" was done with actual scissors and rubber cement. Mike and I would get together with our wives about once a week to fill orders. We'd eat TV dinners, lick stamps and stuff envelopes until the wee hours of the morning.

We tried to keep up our schedule of publishing *Ideas* books on a quarterly schedule, but we averaged around three per year. We sold subscriptions which were good for four issues, no matter how long it took. We never ran out of ideas because youth workers around the country were sending in lots of them. Mike and I would write a few of our own along the way, but the vast majority came from youth workers who responded to our notice in each issue which said "We Just Got Another Great Idea: Yours." We offered to pay anywhere from $5 to $10 per idea (depending on length, not quality) which was more than enough to generate plenty of good ideas. Of course, we rejected the ones we didn't like. The only requirement we had for any idea back then was that it had been "tried and tested" on an actual youth group. We never asked our contributors to sign any kind of release form, nor did we ask for permission to use their idea in other books or resources. We just sent people a check and the deal was done.

Within a few years those *Ideas* books became the lifeblood of Youth Specialties. Later on the organization became better known for events like the National Youth Workers Convention, but for many years the *Ideas* books were the only thing we did that made any money. When we started doing seminars for youth workers around the country, we showcased many of the ideas in our books and sold a ton of them. They weren't sold in bookstores at the time but directly to youth workers by subscriptions and at our events. The "sales pitch" thus became the most important part of our presentations. At the seminar book table whenever someone would buy a whole set of *Ideas* books, we would yell and scream, set off sirens and make a huge deal out of it. Those books sold like hotcakes.

That they were selling so well in the early 1970s didn't go unnoticed by other publishers. An editor at Zondervan Publishing House approached us about repackaging them for the for the Christian bookstore market. We had a pretty dim view of Christian bookstores at that time because they offered nothing at all for youth workers and sold so much of what we called "Jesus Junk." But we liked the sound of what they were offering, so we said yes.

Within a few years, Zondervan published a series of books with titles like *Way Out Ideas for Youth Groups, Far Out Ideas for Youth Groups, Incredible Ideas for Youth Groups, Super Ideas for Youth Groups* and so on. Each of them contained a "best of" collection of ideas from our original *Ideas* books, and they too sold like crazy. Rather than having Youth Specialties' name on the cover, however, they had Mike and me as authors. I always felt a little bit guilty about that, since so many of those ideas came from other youth workers who only got five bucks for their idea. Those Zondervan books really helped us out financially, however, and I still run into people all the time who have copies of those Wayne Rice and Mike Yaconelli books on their shelves.

I suppose the only regret I ever had about putting out all those *Ideas* books back then was that we may have squelched some creativity along the way. I often wondered how many youth workers didn't bother to think very creatively about their youth ministry programming because they had those idea books on the shelf.

ASSUMING TOO MUCH

Our first *Ideas* books were heavy on the fun stuff—the kinds of things Christian publishing companies wouldn't touch at the time because they didn't have a spiritual application. In those days, if you couldn't tie the egg-and-armpit relay to a Bible verse, then it wasn't going to get published by a Christian publisher.

But we had a philosophy of youth ministry that didn't make a distinction between Christian fun and regular fun, the sacred and the secular. It was all the same to us. If fun was being had by Christians, then it was Christian fun. It didn't need a Bible verse or a lesson to go with it.

I remember as a kid going to church roller-skating parties at the local roller rink. I loved those skating parties but I always hated when the pastor would stop the skating and make everybody sit down on the roller rink surface to listen to a fifteen minute devotional. Somehow that devotional made the roller skating party more acceptable to the church, more "sanctified." Unfortunately it also made me hate those devotionals. I was determined to someday put on roller skating parties which didn't include a mandatory devotional. There's nothing wrong with having fun for fun's sake.

So we published lots of ideas for fun and games, assuming that church youth workers would know how to use them appropriately. Neither did we provide too many ideas for teaching the Bible or "lesson plans." We assumed that youth workers already had that material from their churches and didn't really need (or want) us telling them what to teach.

I think we just assumed that most people shared the same ministry philosophy that we had at the beginning—which was to reach teenagers for Christ by creating exciting and interesting youth group meetings and activities. All of the ideas we published were designed with that purpose in mind—from Chubby Bunny to the World's Largest Pillow Fight. We wanted to put on events that kids would tell their friends about and look forward to attending week after week.

Young Life had a different ministry philosophy from Campus Life. They emphasized relationships over programs, but they also needed programs to make the relationships possible. That's how ideas are supposed to work. We still use all kinds of programs and good ideas to fulfill the purposes that we have in mind. Most youth workers are very pragmatic, very bottom line oriented. If they buy a youth ministry book containing both a philosophy of ministry and a collection of ideas at the back of the book, nine out of ten will skip over the first part of the book and go straight for the ideas. (By the way, there are no ideas at the back of *this* book so don't bother looking.) The danger in doing so is that we lose sight of the intention behind the ideas, the purpose behind the programs. There's nothing wrong with programs of any kind so long as there is a good reason for doing them. It's easy however to fall into the trap of doing certain programs just because they've been done before or they've been done successfully somewhere else.

I heard a story about an old church in New England which had beautiful stained glass windows, oak pews, an ornate pulpit and balcony. For many years, this church also had a rather odd tradition during its Sunday morning worship services. During the recitation of the Apostles' Creed, the entire congregation would turn and face the rear of the church. After the reading was over, they would do a complete 180 and turn back around to face the front. No one was quite sure why they did this, but they believed that it was an important and necessary part of their worship tradition.

Finally someone decided to do a little research to find out the origin of the tradition. What they found was that early in the church's history, the original balcony rail at the rear of the sanctuary had the full text of the Apostles' Creed engraved in it. Earlier generations of worshipers turned around simply so they could read the inscription. Even though that inscription was no longer there, the congregation continued the practice of turning around to face the rear of the church.

Some youth ministry programs are a lot like that old church. When I ask them why they do what they do, they aren't really sure except that the previous youth pastor did those same things and the one before him (or her) and so on down the line. My guess is that somebody had a good reason for putting those programs into place, just like we did in the 1960s when we zapped kids with the electric chair or put on a Hootenanny. They may sound a bit ridiculous now, but at the time they met a need and were very effective for accomplishing the purpose for which they were intended.

Many youth ministry writers and bloggers are quick to condemn the "attractional" programs that emerged out of the parachurch youth ministries of the 1950s and 1960s. Some of what was done during that era certainly deserves criticism, but much of it was done for the same reasons youth workers do what they do today. In fact, as you look back over the past five decades, youth workers have consistently tried to create relevant programs to attract teenagers and to keep them connected to the church.

The mistake we made in the past wasn't so much in the *kind* of programs we ran but in our reliance on them to keep kids coming to our youth groups. Programs may keep kids coming, but they won't keep them connected. Truth is, they may even be counter-productive. Ben Patterson warned about this in an article for *Youthworker* more than twenty-five years ago:

> It is a sad fact of life that often the stronger the youth program in the church and the more deeply the young people of the church identify with it, the weaker the chances are that those same young people will remain in the church

when they grow too old for the young program. Why? Because the youth program has become a *substitute* for participation in the church, just as the youth worker has been a substitute parent. When the kids outgrow the youth program, they also outgrow what they have come to know of the church.[4]

THE RIGHT KIND OF PROGRAMS

So should you get rid of all your youth ministry programs? No, probably not if you want to keep your job. But all programs should be evaluated constantly not just based on attendance numbers and popularity with students but on the basis of your theology and philosophy of youth ministry. When you do this, you may find that there are quite a few programs that ought to be eliminated.

I recently consulted with a church that was trying to become more family-friendly and intergenerational. As I began to observe the programs they already had in place, I attended a youth worship service that was held prior to the church's regular adult worship in the sanctuary. As youth worship services go, it was well-attended, and the students who played in the worship band were obviously very talented and loved performing in front of their peers. But there was an obvious (or maybe not-so-obvious) problem here. As successful as this service had been for many years, it undermined the church's goal of bringing families and the generations together. Many of the students who attended the youth service saw no need to attend worship in the main sanctuary where their parents and the older generations worshiped. By comparison, it was pretty boring. Not surprisingly, there was a history of teenagers leaving this church soon after their youth ministry days were over. They either went to a cooler church, started a new church or just dropped out of church altogether. I recommended to this church that it discontinue their youth worship service and instead find ways to integrate their students into the life of the congregation.

Every church and every youth ministry needs programs, but every program should be evaluated and reviewed according to a few key questions.

Does this program support families? Every youth ministry program should in some way strengthen and support families. If it doesn't, or worse, if it has the opposite effect of weakening or undermining families, then it should be discontinued. I realize that not every event has a direct relationship to families, but we should always be thinking about how a program or activity might impact a family's time together, their finances, their relationships with each other and so on.

There are many youth ministry program ideas that will bless, encourage, equip and involve parents in some way. I've written other books full of ideas for doing all of those things. Obviously not every youth ministry program or activity needs to directly include parents. But if you are teaching a youth Bible study or class, just be thinking about how the class can be used to strengthen families and encourage interaction between parents and teens. Every lesson plan or message you give can include "homework" for students which engages parents in some way.

For example, if you are planning a mission trip for your youth group, why not make it a mission trip for families? How many times have we taken kids on mission trips only to have them return home unable to communicate to their parents what they have experienced? I recently went on a family mission trip into Mexico during the height of the "Mexico scare." Because of violence in Mexico and an outbreak of the swine flu, these families went across the border with great fear and trepidation. But their experience together building houses and working with disadvantaged children and families was life-changing for all of them and will likely have a positive impact on those families for years to come.

If your youth ministry is in the habit of taking youth group excursions to theme parks or other attractions, stop before you do the next one and ask yourself whether or not this is the best use of our time. Why am I doing this? Wouldn't it be better for me to spend my time helping parents and families succeed with their kids? Parents should be taking their kids to amusement parks, not the youth pastor. Don't get me wrong; there's a time and a place for fun activities, but they should come in the context of supporting families—as well as connecting teenagers with other adults.

Does this program help to bring teenagers and adults together? For many years I've taught that the primary purpose of youth ministry programs is to give us (adult leaders) a good excuse to hang out with teenagers. Why else would we want to hold a lock-in or burger bash? We all have too much to do anyway. Every event, every activity, every meeting should be designed with relationships in mind. If the event

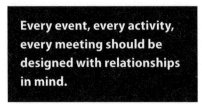

Every event, every activity, every meeting should be designed with relationships in mind.

promotes interactions between teenagers and adult mentors who can encourage them and help them grow in their faith, then it's probably worth doing.

I remember years ago speaking at a youth workers gathering in the Midwest when somebody asked "How can we create a youth ministry program that is run entirely by the teenagers? We want our kids to take *ownership* of their youth ministry, so that they are not so dependent upon the adults of the church to keep it going."

I could hardly believe the question. The concept was completely foreign to me. I struggled for an answer and probably mumbled something to the effect that a youth ministry without adults is not a youth ministry at all. The whole point of youth ministry is to bring adults and teens together so that the faith can be passed on from one generation to the next. If that's not happening, then the youth ministry should be discontinued.

Someone might argue that allowing the teenagers to run their own youth ministry program (without interference from adults) is a good way to prepare youth for leadership roles in the church later on. I would respond that "playing church" as teenagers probably does no more good than "playing house." The only way children learn how to become fully functioning members of a household is to participate in a real family, not a pretend one. I agree that teenagers are capable of assuming leadership roles in the church, but they shouldn't be treated merely as the church of tomorrow. They can be part of the church right now.

Youth ministry programs should bring adults and teens together. And the role of the youth pastor is to equip and train those adults who are willing to come alongside teenagers and be a positive influence on their lives, which they will inevitably do. As my old friend Steve Glenn once put it, "Teenagers left to their own devices always gravitate to the oldest person they can find who will take them seriously and treat them with dignity and respect." Which leads me to the next question we should be asking about programs.

Does this program treat teenagers with respect? Is it encouraging youth to become more engaged as young men and women of the church, or are we simply warehousing them until they "grow up"? Are we treating them more like the young adults they are becoming or more like the children they once were?

There are some adults (and many parents in particular) who believe that the purpose of a youth ministry is to simply keep kids busy and well behaved. Early in my youth ministry career I learned that parents expected me (as the paid youth minister) to not only turn their teenagers into good Christians but to keep them off drugs and alcohol, prevent them from having sex and make sure they stayed away from music with bad lyrics and R-rated movies. They wanted me to provide plenty of wholesome activities for their kids as well as exemplary role models. And make sure they were safe and got home on time.

Parents just can't help themselves. They have this irrepressible urge to control their teenagers rather than helping them grow into capable, self-reliant young men and women who can function on their own. It's an urge that gets carried right over into the expectations they have of the youth ministry. And we youth workers have been more than happy to oblige.

We do our best to provide lots of fun activities and small doses of religious instruction to keep teenagers occupied and out of trouble. Once in a while we show off the youth group in a positive light so that all the parents and adults can applaud and be impressed with the good job we're doing. But what we're actually doing is slowing down (if not preventing altogether) the spiritual formation of these young people and setting them on a clear exit path from the church when they get older.

I believe we can use youth ministry programming to help blend young people into full and complete participation in the life of the church. There's no reason to treat them like children. They are fully capable of "putting away childish things" and taking their place alongside adults in the church. The process of integrating youth into the church will be gradual, and it will mean that the entire congregation will probably have to make some adjustments, but it can and should be done.

I realize that this has been tried in the past without a lot of success. I worked with teenagers in a Lutheran church for several years and learned all about confirmation. It was considered a sacred tradition which for generations had been a very important initiation ceremony—a rite of passage—for Lutheran youth to teach them the key doctrines of Lutheranism and give them entry into full church membership. After confirmation, these young people were considered honorary adults and among other things could now receive communion, having been "confirmed" in the faith.

As I quickly discovered however, most Lutheran youth—while they looked forward to the idea of gaining this new upgraded status in the church—were not very fond of the confirmation process itself. Confirmation had the reputation for being dull and boring. It involved a regimen of instruction by the pastor and memorization of Luther's small catechism, which felt more like cramming for a test than discovering the mysteries and wonders of the Christian faith. The pattern was pretty predictable. Parents would send their kids off to confirmation, and then when they had successfully completed the program and had their confirmation ceremony, they would be graduated right out of the church just like they graduated out of high school. I have a feeling that if we had researchers then like we have today, we would have heard plenty about the alarming drop-out rate among fourteen- and fifteen-year-olds in Lutheran churches.

> **The goal of parenting is not to be a parent anymore. In other words, if you are a parent, you want to work yourself out of a job.**

I was recently asked by a church to speak to their middle school Sunday school class. When I arrived at the classroom, I noticed there were no chairs in the room, except for a few around the edges. When I asked the adult leaders about it, they said, "Oh, we never set up chairs. The kids just sit on the floor." The adults in the room sat in the chairs around the perimeter.

I wanted to ask the adults a second question (I didn't): "How would you feel if you showed up at a meeting and there were no chairs? If you were expected to sit on the floor, would that make you feel more like an adult . . . or more like a child?" I think we should be asking similar questions of all the programming we do for teenagers. Programming is not neutral. It can either help us accomplish our goals and objectives or it can undermine them.

STAGES OF PROGRAMMING

Let me draw a comparison between programming and parenting. The goal of parenting is not to be a parent anymore. In other words, if you are a parent, you want to work yourself out of a job. This sometimes comes as a shock to parents. At Understanding Your Teenager seminars I teach that "your child's adolescence marks the beginning of your own obsolescence." This is illustrated by the *five stages of parenting*:

- Stage One (0-2): Catering. During a child's first two years, he or she discovers that parents are there to take care of their every need. They begin to think, *The world revolves around me!*

- Stage Two (2-10): Controlling. Now it's time for parents to establish their absolute authority over the child and for the child to learn absolute obedience. This can best be described as a "benevolent dictatorship."

- Stage Three (10-14): Coaching. As the young adolescent begins his or her transition to adulthood, parents can now "let out some rope" while still retaining their authority and setting limits.

- Stage Four (14-18): Consulting. During adolescence, smart parents avoid "micro-managing" their teens by giving them more and more control over their own lives. They still set limits and allow teens to learn from their mistakes by experiencing consequences.

- Stage Five (18-on): Caring. The last stage is when parents realize that their job as a parent is over. It's time for the young adult to start living on his or her own, even if they are still at home, with the least amount of interference as possible. All the parent can do is care (pray!) and remain available as a mentor and friend.

In a sense, this is what is called *weaning*, and as Yaconelli used to say, "weaning has never been easy—for the weaner or the weanee!" What makes it so difficult is that most parents have a hard time transitioning from the controlling stage (of childhood) to the coaching or consulting stages (of adolescence). In other words, parents keep treating their teenagers like children, which invariably leads to conflict and rebellion, and seriously retards their development into capable, self-reliant adults.

There are parallels here in how we treat young people in the church. When we limit their options for participation and involvement in the church, we discourage them and set them up for rebellion. From the nursery to the adult ministries of the church, we generally divide ministries along the same lines as the five stages of parenting anyway. If we also have as a goal to help parents raise adult followers of Jesus rather than infantilized adults, our programming might look something like this:

- Stage One (nursery): Parents are responsible for their children, but the church is there to provide support, parenting education, childcare during worship times, baby dedication, baptism or christening services and so on.

- Stage Two (children's ministry): Parents are encouraged, taught and given the tools to pass their faith on to their children at home. The children's ministry and family ministries of the church are there to encourage parents, equip them and reinforce what they are teaching in the home with graded classes and other children's programs at the church.

- Stage Three (middle school ministry): Parents are encouraged and equipped to pass faith on to their children at home. The middle school ministry exists to reinforce what students are learning at home, provide rites of passage into church membership, surround them with mentors and give them an introduction to the adult ministries of the church.

- Stage Four (high school ministry): Parents are encouraged to stay connected with their teens and to have faith conversations at home. The youth ministry of the church can also provide programs that encourage parent-teen dialogue as well as intergenerational activities which begin to integrate teens more fully into the life of the church.

- Stage Five (adult ministries): Students take their place alongside other adult members of the congregation as leaders, lifetime learners and committed followers of Jesus.

If we have a holistic strategy such as this for the entire church, then we can provide effective programs in all of our ministries for integrating children and youth into the life of the church. Such a framework, coupled with a comprehensive plan for systematically passing on the core stories, beliefs and values of the Christian faith in partnership with parents, could be a significant step forward towards helping young people grow into mature adult followers of Jesus.

GOING BIG TIME
Thinking About Youth Workers

Oh Lord, you know, many years ago
I said I'd do anything for you.
Then sure enough, you called my bluff
and showed me just what to do.
Now I hate to complain, but I'm needin' a change.
Could you find somebody else to use?
'Cause like it or not, I think I've got
those Gettin' Out of Youth Work Blues.

In 1973, to celebrate my tenth anniversary in youth work, I wrote "Gettin' Out of Youth Work Blues." I'd sing it at youth worker events in the style of Johnny Cash's "A Boy Named Sue" (kind of a country rap), and it was always good for a few laughs. The verses had to do with growing old and irrelevant in youth ministry—something every youth worker could relate to. We all knew our youth ministry days were going to be numbered. The turnover rate for youth workers in the church at that time was still pretty high.

There's a now debunked urban legend about youth ministry longevity which has the average stay of a youth worker in one church at about eighteen months (after which they end up in an asylum—ba-dum-bum). Mike and I probably helped lend credibility to that statistic. In the fall of 1969, Mike quit his youth ministry position at the Baptist church after only one year and took a full-time job with a company called Jack Young and Associates, a San Diego investment firm specializing in tax shelters. Jack was a Christian businessman who heard Mike give a speech at a meeting of the local Toastmasters Club. Mike had been a member of Toastmasters for several years and had even won a national speech contest sponsored by the organization. Although he knew nothing about the investment business, Mike was hired on the spot to sell tax shelters to rich people.

I definitely had misgivings about Mike taking this job. The only thing that made sense about it was the paycheck. I remember how amazed I was when I found out how much Mike was going to get paid. He was not only going to get what was at that time a large salary but a company car to boot—not coincidentally a brand new Corvette. Quite honestly I was worried about Mike, that the money might corrupt him or that he would get so busy selling tax shelters that he wouldn't have time for Youth Specialties. Neither of those things turned out to be true, although we did notice some large men in Italian suits who were always following him around.

Jack Young was very fond of Mike and extremely supportive of what we were trying to do with Youth Specialties. He gave Mike all the time off he needed and even offered to give us free space on the fourth floor of his office building in downtown San Diego. It housed a bank and the city's local business newspaper on the first floor—definitely in the heart of the coat-and-tie district. Jack's offices were on the eighth floor and

Mike had a very nice office with a view of the city.

I still had a youth ministry job at the Nazarene church (with no office) and a diploma from San Diego State (giving me a little more time) so we decided to take Jack up on his offer. We bought a desk, chair and file cabinet and moved into our new office.[1] We started out with two employees—me plus a secretary who also served as receptionist, typist and shipping manager. Mike didn't draw a salary from YS for another year or two, thanks largely to the generosity of Jack Young.

We wore coats and ties to work back in those days, not just because that was the dress code of the building we were in, but because we wanted to make a statement about youth ministry. We thought of ourselves as *professionals* doing *professional* work. We were getting tired of the question (especially from our wives) "When are you going to get a *real* job?" In our view, we had a real job, one that deserved a coat and tie.

Mike (l.) and I in ties, demonstrating a game from *Ideas*

The professionalizing of youth ministry had already begun with parachurch ministries like Youth for Christ and Young Life, but when Mike and I made the transition from parachurch youth ministry to church-based youth ministry in the 1960s, it didn't take long for us to learn that youth workers in the church didn't get the same kind of respect we got at Youth for Christ.

This may not have been typical of all YFC programs, but in San Diego those of us who wore those snappy orange blazers issued to Campus Life staff were held in pretty high regard by just about everybody—pastors, city officials, teachers and school administrators, business leaders in the community. We were invited to preach in local churches, give invocations at graduation ceremonies, lead chapel services for our professional (or not so professional) sports teams and appear on local TV shows as experts on youth issues. We also had lots of role models—people who had risen up in the ranks of YFC and become well known as leaders in the evangelical movement.

So our move to church youth ministry was something of a real downer for both of us. Suddenly we were in a junior profession which no one expected would be more than a temporary stop on the way to becoming a real pastor. Of course to become a real pastor, you needed to go to seminary, and both Mike and I were dead set against that. Our impression was that seminary deprogrammed you from any call you might have to youth ministry. Everyone we knew who had completed seminary was no longer in youth work. Of course, you couldn't really blame them. Working with youth in the church in those days was just a cut above the church janitor, although the church janitor had a bigger office and probably a bigger paycheck.

Youth ministry was still considered an apprenticeship, a temporary stop on the way to "real ministry." We wanted to change all that.

THE NATIONAL YOUTH WORKERS CONVENTION

After moving Youth Specialties to its new downtown office, we began to dream a little bit more about how we could elevate the profession of youth ministry. Both Mike and I had attended several denominational conferences and Sunday school conventions where we had tried to sell our *Ideas* books, and we were always amazed by how little attention these conferences gave to youth ministry. We were also amazed by just how boring those conferences were.

So early in 1970, we decided to put on our own convention. We began writing down ideas for what we thought would be the coolest convention in the history of the world. All of the speakers would be top notch and all of the seminars would be about working with teenagers. This had never been done before, at least not that we knew of, and we just knew it was going to be incredible.

We decided to call it the National Youth Workers Convention, which was rather presumptuous, since we really didn't expect anyone to come from outside California. When we announced our plans to put on a national youth ministry convention to friends and family, the most common response we got was "Yeah, right," if not outright laughter. But we were dreaming big and could not be deterred.

One person who *did* like our idea was Jack Young, who insisted that he loan us the money to book the hotel, print and mail our advertising, and cover our other expenses. We were obviously buoyed by this and promised to pay him back. We had decided early on that we wanted to hold our convention in a nice hotel—a place where other professionals hold conferences. We wanted youth workers to feel special, like they were important, doing important work. Up to this time, the only youth worker conferences we knew about required attendees to bring a sleeping bag, take cold showers and eat bad camp food. We wanted to make a statement: pastors went to conventions in convention hotels and so could we. We were professionals, and we wanted to hold a professional convention in a professional place.

So we made arrangements at a popular resort hotel on Mission Bay in San Diego, called the Bahia. We asked a good friend of ours, Denny Rydberg, to serve as our "convention coordinator." Denny had recently moved from Washington to San Diego to become youth director at First Presbyterian Church; he seemed to us to be about the most organized person we knew. He had a personal calendar that was about the size of a phone book and did seminars on time management. He was a godsend to us because we couldn't pay him anything. He agreed to help us with that first convention and the following year joined our staff full time.

With Denny on the team, we started booking every speaker we could think of who might have something worthwhile to say to youth workers. Most of them were friends from our YFC days or people we had heard speak at other events. The lineup for our first convention included Joseph Bayly, John MacArthur Jr., Mel White, Lyman Coleman and about twenty others. For music, we lined up folk singer Sonny Salsbury and composer Ralph Carmichael.[2] We advertised the convention by placing ads in magazines like *Eternity, Faith at Work, Campus Life* and *Christianity Today.* We also mailed brochures to several thousand names we had been collecting from selling *Ideas* books.

We had no idea if anyone would show up. We were worried because our registration rates were higher than most youth workers were used to paying ($35) and the hotel rooms were expensive at $16 a night. With a month to go, advance registrations weren't too encouraging. But a week or so before the convention, we got a surge of last minute registrations and ended up with around three hundred attendees, which we considered a success even though we lost a lot of money. Actually we lost a lot of Jack Young's money, but after the convention was over, he told us to start planning another convention and forgave the debt.[3]

Most of the attendees were from California, as we expected they would be. Noticeably absent at that first convention were women. The only woman speaker was Marilee Zdenek, an actress and dancer from Hollywood Presbyterian Church who led a seminar on how to incorporate dance and drama into a worship service—a pretty revolutionary concept back in those days. I can't say for sure, but other than wives I don't remember any other women being at that first convention. Youth ministry was still basically a boys club in 1970.

THINKING ABOUT YOUTH PASTORS

One of my favorite jokes is about a husband and wife, both of them sixty years old, who were celebrating their wedding anniversary. Someone gave them a magic lantern as a gift. Sure enough, when they rubbed the lantern a genie popped out and announced that they each would get one wish—anything they wanted.

The wife went first. "I've never been on a cruise before," she said. "I'd love to go on a cruise with my husband." Poof! Two tickets for an around-the-world cruise instantly appeared in her hands.

The husband then made his wish. "Well, if I'm going to go on a cruise with my wife . . . I wish I was married to someone thirty years younger than me!" Poof! He instantly became ninety years old.

Of course the moral of this story is, *Be careful what you wish for.*

It's hard today to remember a time when youth workers in the church weren't considered professionals. While we still suffer from a few image problems and have some salary inequities to overcome, there's no question that today's youth workers are better trained, better equipped and held in much higher esteem than ever before. The stereotypical youth worker who carries a game book in one hand and a referee's whistle in the other has definitely left the building.

By some estimates, there are now more than sixty thousand

full-time youth pastors serving in churches all across North America.[4] There are dozens of professional youth ministry conferences held in major convention centers and hotels every year. The National Network of Youth Ministries has several thousand members, and almost every major Christian publisher now offers a line of youth ministry books. The National Association of Youth Ministry Educators was formed a few years ago by a growing group of youth ministry professors from colleges and theological seminaries around the world, and they now publish an academic journal featuring scholarly treatises on youth ministry. Add to that the several hundred cottage industries that have emerged recently to provide resources for youth pastors, and it's safe to say that youth ministry is no longer a junior profession.

When I travel the country conducting parent seminars, I'm sometimes amazed by the investment that many churches have made in their youth ministries. Not only have they hired a professional staff, but they have provided them with multimillion-dollar youth centers complete with meeting space, classrooms, basketball courts, video game lounges, coffee houses (with free Internet access), and a suite of offices that would rival any you would find anywhere.

So our wish came true. The calling of youth ministry has been given the validation and legitimacy that we wanted so badly forty years ago. But questions are now being raised: Are we doing *better* youth ministry now than we did in the past? Are we getting better results now than in the past?

Quite honestly, I don't think we have the answers to those questions right now. With all of its advances, youth ministry is still in its infancy. The research that is being done now can't be compared with similar research from decades ago simply because none exists. Personally, I believe youth ministry *is* much better than it was when I began doing it in the 1960s simply because it has benefited from four decades of experience and innovation. I'm convinced that the quality, the dedication and the passion of the men and women who are doing youth ministry today far exceeds that of my generation of youth workers. There's no doubt in my mind that youth ministry's best days certainly lie ahead.

One reason why I believe this is because today's youth workers can learn from all the mistakes we have already made. And one of those mistakes certainly has to do with taking youth ministry out of the hands of literally millions of parents and other unpaid adults in the church who previously organized and led their church's youth ministries with great effectiveness.

THE PROBLEM OF PROFESSIONALISM

When I attend a National Youth Workers Convention today, I'm always amazed by how many resources confront you when you enter the exhibit hall. There are more booths in the exhibit hall now than we had attendees at our first convention. And I can say that with few exceptions (the bobble-head dashboard Jesus dolls come to mind) the quality gets better every year. There truly are some outstanding resources being produced today to help us all do better youth ministry.

A few years ago, I took a businessman friend of mine to one of the National Youth Workers Conventions and walked him around the convention center. After a stroll down a few of the aisles he commented, "I had no idea this was such a big industry. Obviously working with teenagers is a lot more complicated than I thought." What was an encouragement to me as a professional was actually a discouragement to him, a layperson. He saw all the conferences and seminars and resources as one more reason why he was completely unqualified to work with students.

Today, even in churches without a youth pastor, it's hard to find anyone who is willing to take on the responsibility for working with the youth. Why is this? The answer for many is that they simply *don't feel qualified.*

With all the books and training events on youth ministry these days, who has time to read or attend them all? How do you know which approach is best? What's the difference between purpose-driven youth ministry, family-based youth ministry, presence-centered youth ministry and youth ministry 3.0? Where do you start? What do you have to know? How many degrees do you need? Youth ministry has become a job for professionals; everybody knows that it takes special skills and training to do it properly. There are so many books to read and conferences to attend. That's why so many churches—rather than asking parents or volunteers to work with their kids—desperately seek help from anyone they can find who seems *qualified* to work with their youth. They place ads on the Youth Specialties website or post them on the walls of local seminaries and colleges hoping to find someone—*anyone*—who knows something about youth ministry and who also needs a job.

Certainly the outsourcing of ministry in the church is nothing new. Since the days of the early church, congregations have eagerly handed the ministry of the church off to pastors and priests, believing that they were the only ones qualified to preach, teach and administer the sacraments. This is not really a new problem.

Add to this that most adults feel pretty insecure about working with teenagers to begin with. They aren't sure the kids will like them. They don't keep up with youth culture. They're afraid they'll say something stupid. They know that teenagers are obsessed with coolness, and few adults feel very cool anymore. They don't naturally gravitate toward hanging out with teenagers in the first place, and now we've convinced them that they aren't qualified either. So the volunteer pool gets even smaller.

I've heard some experts on the family lay serious guilt trips on parents by accusing them of outsourcing the spiritual training of their children to professionals, but I think this is unfair. If I were a parent (again), and if I wanted the best for my kids, and if I knew there was a professional pastor on the staff who knew how to help teenagers grow spiritually and was being paid by my tithes and offerings to do it, I would certainly want to take advantage of that and make sure my kids were there. Before we blame parents for not being more involved in the spiritual training of their kids or beat up the rest of the congregation for their unwillingness to serve as volunteers, maybe we need to reinvent the role of the youth pastor a little bit.

OF LIGHT BULBS AND PIED PIPERS

Early in my youth ministry career I heard Jay Kesler describe what he called the "bright young man" model of youth ministry. He compared youth workers with light bulbs. Just as light bulbs attract bugs, so *bright young men* (sorry, there were no women youth pastors in those days) attract teenagers. Every congregation needed a bright young man to keep the kids buzzing around the church.

The bright young man (or woman) model of youth ministry has been a popular one, repeated by thousands of churches over the years to keep their youth groups stocked with kids. It worked great except that as we all know, light bulbs burn out frequently. Whenever a youth pastor would leave, the bugs (teenagers) disappeared. So the church would have to go out and find another light bulb, another bright young man or woman with enough charisma and youth appeal to bring the kids back.

Another image of youth workers comes from the famous Pied Piper of Hamelin. If you're not familiar with the story, here are the Cliff's notes. A small town (Hamelin) had a rat infestation problem and a man dressed in pied (multicolored) clothing showed up claiming to be a rat-catcher. The people of the town agreed to pay him a fair amount if he would rid their town of rats. So one day he played his musical pipe (something like a bagpipe) and the rats followed him out of town and into the river where they all drowned.

The people of Hamelin were very pleased with this outcome, but they refused to pay the piper for his service (which is where we get the term "It's time to pay the piper"). To get revenge, the "pied piper" came back into town *while all the villagers were in church*. This time the music from his pipe attracted all the children of the village, who followed him out of town and into a cave where they were never heard from again. They simply disappeared.

The problem of disappearing teenagers has been a growing one for churches across the United States. While we've been in church, the youth have been following their youth pastors into a cave somewhere. Kara Eckmann Powell of the Fuller Youth Institute reports on some new research that has been done with teenagers who are members of church youth groups. Her studies have found that "youth leaders" top the list of reasons why teens attend their youth groups. They aren't there for the activities and the fun and games and delicious pizza, they come because they admire their youth pastors or other adults who lead the group.[5] This of course is very affirming and encouraging news for youth workers, but it's not very encouraging news for the church or for parents. If a young person's primary connection to the church is their youth pastor, what do you think is going to happen when the youth pastor leaves? This fragile and frequently broken connection can cause serious damage to a young person's relationship with the church.

In his book *Faith Begins at Home* Mark Holmen writes,

> Pied pipers are usually gifted in working with children or teens but simply don't have the interest or desire to bridge their ministry to the home. Through their dynamic and charismatic leadership, they're able to draw a crowd of students to follow them. Yet in many cases, Pied Pipers see parents as a disruption to the work they're trying to do. Unfortunately they don't realize that their success or influence is only temporary.[6]

I know it's hard to resist playing the role of the pied piper or the "bright young" youth minister. Most of us like being the center of attention, having young people look up to us, follow us around and treat us like rock stars. Many senior pastors fall into the same trap. We all know of churches that are built on the preaching gifts and personality of celebrity pastors who can fill the pews. The early church apparently had a bright young man problem of its own. Paul warned the church at Corinth to get their eyes off of personalities like himself, Apollos and Peter but to instead focus on Christ. "God didn't send me out to collect a following for myself," he wrote, "but to preach the Message of what he has done, collecting a following for him" (1 Corinthians 1:17 *The Message*). Youth ministries that are built upon the personality and charisma of a gifted youth pastor are almost certain to collapse when he or she moves on.

THE YOUTH PASTOR AS EQUIPPER

So should we get rid of all the youth pastors? Of course not. Youth pastors who have been called by God to love on teenagers and help them to become lifelong followers of Jesus are still desperately needed for the day and age in which we live. But we may need to reinvent the role of the youth pastor or maybe even give the position a new name. Youth pastors have become so well-known for their roles as bright young men and pied pipers, there may be too much baggage that comes with the title.

I've heard it said that the problem with being a youth pastor is that your job description is limited by your title: you are a pastor to youth and that's all. But a youth pastor's role is much larger than that. Youth pastors—like all pastors—are to be "equippers of the saints for the work of ministry" (Ephesians 4:12). I think the mistake we've made in the past is that we have equated the *saints* in this passage with the *youth*.

Most youth ministry mission statements that I've seen includes a line or two about equipping young people for works of service or helping them to become student leaders. That's a good thing of course, but I believe that the primary role of the youth pastor today should be focused more on equipping adults rather than teenagers. If we truly want better long-term results and a youth ministry that won't collapse when we leave, we must learn to work with adults—especially parents.

I sometimes ask struggling youth pastors to write down for me what their schedule looks like in a typical week. More often than not they record such things as "spent time on campus with students," "played video games with students," "hung out at the mall with students," "met several students at Starbucks," "played some hoops with students," and so on. Their list usually also includes a Bible study or two and several other youth group activities. But it doesn't take long to see what's wrong with this picture.

What if youth pastors divided their time more equally among students and their parents? What if a third of their time was dedicated to students, another third with parents or adults, the remaining third of their time with all of them together? If that were to happen, a youth pastor would be spending the majority of his or her time encouraging adults who have way more influence over their teenagers than he or she does.

I realize that many youth workers feel completely unqualified to help parents in any way and raise lots of objections. But there are lots of resources available (including a book I've written myself on the topic).[7] We can find the people and the resources we need to help parents stay connected with their kids and help them grow in their faith. If we can equip parents with the tools they need to become better parents, we're more likely to see a turnaround in those church drop-out numbers that have been plaguing us in recent years.

We don't have to be the heroes. What we want to do instead is equip the people who are already most connected to the teenagers in our youth group so that they can continue the work of ministry long after we are gone. There is no doubt in my mind now after forty years of youth ministry that the only teenagers I wish I had spent more time with as a youth pastor are my own. They are the ones I love most and care about most. I also wish I had spent more time helping other parents take advantage of the crucial roles they play in the lives of their kids. Had I done so, I'm sure that many more of the youth who were in my youth groups would still be following Jesus today.

In his book *Sustainable Youth Ministry*, Mark DeVries reminds youth pastors that

> the short-term, high-number, razzle-dazzle success of your current youth ministry might blind you to the fact that success in youth ministry is measured in decades, not in year-to-date comparisons with last year's mediocre youth staffer who, quite honestly, just didn't have your gifts.[8]

This is something most youth workers don't realize until long after their youth ministry days are over.

THE YOUTH PASTOR AS SHEPHERD

Youth pastors are real pastors. I only say that because not everyone thinks of a youth pastor as a real pastor. Youth pastors are often viewed as youth activity directors or perhaps as pastors-in-training with mini-congregations comprised mainly of teenagers. But youth pastors are not just pastors of the youth group. The calling of youth pastor should carry with it an implied shepherding role that is much bigger than keeping a youth ministry program up and running.

The word *pastor* itself comes from the world of herding sheep. Besides the obvious duties pastors have of preaching and teaching the Word of God, administering the sacraments and equipping the saints, it's helpful to remember that pastors are shepherds who shepherd flocks (Acts 20:28).

Youth pastors are shepherds just like senior pastors. I think the assumption is naturally made that a youth pastor's "flock"

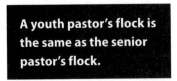

A youth pastor's flock is the same as the senior pastor's flock.

is the youth of the church. But the youth group is not a flock unto itself. It's part of a larger flock which is made up of the entire congregation. A youth pastor's flock is the same as the senior pastor's flock and, in larger churches, all the other pastors of the church. A youth pastor's special responsibility, however, is to keep an eye out for the youth *who are part of that flock.*

Think of an actual flock of sheep out on a pasture somewhere. There will never be a time when *all* of the young sheep are intentionally segregated from the rest of the flock. One or two might wander off, but usually they are quickly herded back to safety by the shepherd or by one of the adult sheep. If all the young sheep were to wander off and get separated from the flock, panic would break out in the flock and there would likely be a stampede. Meanwhile, the young sheep are more vulnerable to being eaten by wolves. I don't want to stretch this analogy too far, but my point here is that separating the young sheep from the flock is dangerous.

This has implications for our understanding of a youth pastor's role in a local church. For one thing, they should have a seat at the table of leadership in the church. I'm always amazed how many decisions are made in churches without any regard at all for the opinions and special needs of young people. Many youth leave the institutional church because they don't feel like they are part of it. They don't have a voice. In their view, churches are run by old people who really don't have any idea what young people are like or how they feel. Dan Kimball asks

> How easy is it for a young leader to be in a place of influence and innovation in the church? This is an important question, because if you aren't creating ways for younger people to be shapers and influencers and to bring innovative ideas, you will squelch their hearts and minds and only reinforce the idea that we are a hierarchical organized religion.[9]

When a youth pastor is part of the leadership of the church, he or she can not only be a voice for emerging generations but can provide opportunities for other young people to get involved and to have a voice in the church as well. A youth pastor can become an advocate for youth to the whole church. If he or she is considered a shepherd with special responsibility and love for the adolescents of the flock, he or she can been a cheerleader for students, an advocate for youth, someone who keeps the rest of the church mindful of the fact that teenagers need their encouragement, acceptance, wisdom, time and attention.

When I was a youth pastor, I think most people saw my job as providing teenagers with a program of their own, a way of getting the kids out of the adults' hair. I would submit that a youth pastor's job today is just the opposite: bringing the generations together again as a way of getting the kids back *into* the adults' hair. Youth pastors are shepherds who help keep the flock together and moving in the same direction.

LONG LIVE LONGEVITY

The position of youth pastor is notoriously one with a lot of turnover. Pied pipers can only play the pipe for so long. You just run out of wind.

I can't tell you how many youth pastors I've counseled over the years, on the verge of quitting, who find themselves questioning their call, struggling with their identities, feeling anxious about the future and looking over the fence at greener pastures. Even though they gave the best years of their lives to working with kids, they somehow ended up wondering if they made the right decision all those many years ago.

Some found themselves involuntarily retired from their youth ministry positions because the church decided to bring on a younger (less expensive) youth pastor to give the youth ministry a "shot in the arm." Others just felt they had lost a step in youth ministry as they got older and were losing the passion for youth ministry they once had. More likely they had just lost their passion for lock-ins, cold pizza and broken-down church buses. Some youth workers find that youth ministry just can't support them financially anymore. They'd love to stay in youth work but they also need to feed their families.

Sadly this is not an uncommon experience for youth workers

who bought into our early vision of youth ministry as a career. When we assured youth workers that youth ministry was not a stepping stone to becoming a senior pastor, many of them took us seriously. They never even considered doing anything else.

Some youth workers I've known have felt a bit stranded. Not having completed their education, they weren't qualified to "move up." They couldn't use youth ministry as a stepping stone even if they wanted to. I have a good friend who left youth ministry to become a planner of parties and special events for corporations. He was definitely qualified to do that.

Other aging youth workers do become senior pastors or take other leadership positions in the church, like missions pastors, executive pastors, small group pastors and the like. I know several former youth pastors who are now surprisingly having success as pastors of senior adults. I've been told that working with junior highers and working with seniors has a lot in common.

Some youth workers plant new churches of their own, often replicating the youth ministries they once led. Some of the largest churches in the country were in fact founded by former youth pastors. And then there are those youth pastors who have extended their careers by becoming youth ministry entrepreneurs in much the same way Mike and I did before them, starting up ministries or businesses to leverage their experience and skill as writers, speakers, consultants or youth ministry experts. Organizations like Simply Youth Ministry, Youth Ministry Architects, YouthSource and Live It Forward are examples of this. The Internet has made it possible (and a whole lot easier) for entrepreneurs to start new ministries which serve youth workers and the church.

But there aren't too many people who remain in the position of youth pastor beyond their thirties and forties, probably because there is still a serious disconnect between longevity in youth ministry and the skill set most people think is required to do it for more than just a few years.

When I started out in youth ministry, I had that skill set. I was young, I could play the guitar (mandatory), tell jokes, lead games, act in funny skits and keep the kids hanging around long enough to teach them some Bible lessons. I had the right look for my era—stylishly long hair with sideburns (and for a while, muttonchops), bell-bottom pants, flowery polyester shirts with pointy collars, patent leather high heel boots. Today you would never want someone who looked like this hanging around your kids.

But as we all know, you don't stay cool forever. The same students who idolized you a week ago can turn on you in a flash and suddenly you find yourself about as cool as a pair of parachute pants. That's when many youth workers start thinking about transitioning into a new ministry or going into the corporate party-planning business.

That's an urge and a trend that needs some serious pushback. If God called you into youth ministry, this is not the time to quit. As a matter of fact, this might be the perfect time to start doing some *really effective* youth ministry. A little gray hair may make you think your stock is fading with teenagers; it's not, but it is definitely rising with parents and other adults in the church. I can say that my most productive years as a youth worker have come in the second half of my youth ministry career. It's unfortunate that so many very gifted youth workers don't stay with it long enough to experience that second half.

Obviously God can call us to do anything he wants us to do. Not all youth pastors are meant to stay in youth work forever. How and where we serve God is not really our decision to make. I sometimes hear from former youth pastors who feel a bit guilty because they moved on to become a senior pastor or take some other job in the church. But there's no reason to feel guilty if you are confident that God was leading you to move on. It's obvious to me that part of God's overall plan for effective youth ministry has been to move some former youth pastors into senior pastor positions and other leadership roles. This will make things much easier for youth pastors of the future.

But the most effective youth workers I know are older now, with enough seasoning and experience to have easy access and credibility with parents and older adults as well as with students. Teenagers don't have a problem with age so long as they are treated respectfully. Neither age nor coolness should have any bearing on one's qualifications for youth ministry leadership.

I don't want to give the impression here that only "well aged" youth pastors can be effective. On the contrary, I know that God regularly uses younger people to accomplish amazing things for the kingdom. Age is no guarantee that anyone has either the calling, maturity or the competence to lead a youth ministry. But because youth ministry of the future will require the ability to connect with and mobilize older adults, age can be a tremendous asset.

It may take time to rid ourselves completely of the "bright young man" stereotype for youth workers in the church, but I'm holding out for the day when I will no longer be asked the question "Aren't you a little old to still be hanging out with teenagers?"

FORWARD MOMENTUM

In November 1970, as soon as the first convention was over, we started making plans for our second. At the top of our wish list for speakers was the renowned author and theologian Francis A. Schaeffer. Schaeffer had achieved rock-star status among young evangelicals, especially with young members of the "Jesus Movement" which was in full swing at this time. Both Mike and

I had read *The God Who Is There, Escape from Reason* and *The Mark of the Christian* and had become big Schaeffer devotees. Mike even traveled to Switzerland where Schaeffer had established a haven for young intellectuals called L'Abri Fellowship. When Mike invited him to come speak to our convention, he declined on the grounds that he was only making one trip to the United States that year. But Mike was persistent and refused to take no for an answer. Finally Schaeffer relented and agreed to make a second trip to the States. The clincher, I think, was when we invited Schaeffer's wife Edith to also be one of our speakers.

With Schaeffer in place as our keynote speaker, our second National Youth Workers Convention at the Sheraton Hotel in San Diego not only attracted more youth workers but a lot more media attention. Other speakers that year included Hal Lindsey and Larry Richards, along with musical performances by Larry Norman, Randy Stonehill and Barry McGuire.[10] We also invited a famous neuroscientist to speak at that convention. Mike and I heard Dr. Robert Tschirgi give an incredible lecture at San Diego State University on the subject of youth culture and ethics. We were pretty impressed and booked him for one of our morning general sessions. We found out later that he was not a Christian but a devotee of Zoroastrianism. His convention talk was not on youth culture and ethics but on technology, science and the future of the human race. "Ultimately, our hope is not in God but in human ingenuity and science," he said to room full of stunned youth workers. After Tschirgi finished his speech and walked off the platform to dead silence, we didn't know what to say. We closed the session in prayer and dismissed everybody for elective seminars. But both Mike and I felt like idiots, blaming each other for not properly vetting this guy. People were angry and some of our attendees (and speakers) were actually threatening to leave.

As it turned out, Tschirgi's speech was a perfect table-setter for Francis Schaeffer. Schaeffer never heard Tschirgi speak because he was taking a nap, trying to sleep off his jet lag from Switzerland. But a few hours later, Schaeffer addressed almost point-by-point every issue that Tschirgi raised. It was pure luck, but everyone at the convention began to believe that we had planned the whole thing. "A stroke of genius," they said, and of course we didn't deny it, although we had no way of knowing what either of those men were going to say. We knew that God was watching over us.

The Tschirgi-Schaeffer incident made us start planning along those lines from then on. We tried to book speakers at our conventions who could offer differing or even contrasting viewpoints on the same subject. Not only did we want to expose our attendees to a wide range of ideas and personalities, but we wanted our convention to be known for its unpredictability and edginess. Other conventions held to a party line, but we wanted to bring lots of different people and ideas together so that we could all learn from each other. One year we changed the name to "The Unconventional Convention" just to emphasize the idea that we were not like other conventions. Nobody quite got the point, however, so we changed it back the next year.[11]

After a couple of years the National Youth Workers Convention started living up to its name. Youth workers were coming from all over the United States and a few other countries as well. Attendance steadily grew, and after four years in San Diego, we moved it to Chicago in 1974 and then to Atlanta in 1975. One great memory of that first Atlanta convention was hearing Tony Campolo speak for the first time. Tony had been recommended to us by Rich Van Pelt, a youth worker from New York who would later become one of our closest friends and colleagues. According to Rich, Campolo was "a very smart version of Yaconelli," which sounded intriguing, so we took a chance and booked him sight unseen.

Tony delivered one of the all-time great opening session talks I've ever heard. Not only did he receive a standing ovation, but the convention floor was buzzing afterward. Everyone wanted to know "Where did you find this guy?" Tony became a great friend and a fixture at all our conventions after that. To this day, I don't think he has missed speaking to at least one of the several YS conventions held each year. Tony says we launched his ministry as a professional speaker. Whether that's true or not is certainly debatable—he surely would have become one of the most popular and controversial voices in the church without our help. I think it's safe to say, however, that the National Youth Workers Convention did help launch the ministry careers of many other well known youth ministry personalities and ministries. Especially after we expanded to two, then three cities per year, the NYWC became the make-or-break showcase and marketing opportunity every year for literally hundreds of organizations, ministries and Christian artists serving the youth ministry industry.

Like I said, we got our wish.

6

NAILING IT TO THE DOOR
Thinking About the Church

I don't blame the board of First Nazarene Church for demanding my resignation. I probably would have fired me too. Parents were unhappy that their kids were being exposed to worldly influences (by me). The church janitor was tired of having to remove Silly String from the shag carpet in the fellowship hall. The church treasurer didn't understand why surfboard wax should qualify as a legitimate youth ministry expense. The pastor was weary of having to pause his sermons for uprisings in the church balcony. And then there was what became known as the "smoking-gun incident."

Actually, it wasn't a smoking gun. It was a smoking guest speaker. During a moment of temporary insanity I invited Mike Yaconelli to speak at one of our youth events. Mike already had somewhat of a "reputation," so some of our church board members attended the event. Things started out really well, but suddenly in the middle of Mike's talk, he nonchalantly lit up a cigarette and took a puff. I was just as surprised as anyone, mainly because Mike didn't smoke. But there he was, in the church building, preaching away with a lit Marlboro between his fingers.

There were no laws about smoking in public places back then, but smoking in a Nazarene church—you may as well have taken off your clothes and stood there stark naked. But Mike kept on preaching while occasionally blowing smoke rings into the air. I was starting to get really worried. After a minute or two of this (which seemed like an hour) the coughing and choking and the waves of consternation in the room forced Mike to stop his message, put out his cigarette and explain himself. "How many of you can tell me what I said after I started smoking the cigarette?" he asked. No one responded; they were still in shock and didn't hear his question, let alone what he said while he was smoking. "See? Just as my cigarette was a distraction and kept you from hearing anything I had to say, we do the same thing to young people when they come into our churches with their long hair, sandals, blue jeans and peace signs. We don't listen to anything they have to say because we don't like the fact that they don't wear underarm deodorant!"

It wasn't a bad object lesson, actually, but it was totally lost on those Nazarenes and only became one more good reason to fire me. Mike apologized, but the pastor called me into his office and asked for my resignation.

THE JESUS MOVEMENT

At that time the Jesus Movement was in full swing around Southern California and thousands of young people were coming to Christ. What began as a kind of spiritual awakening in the Haight-Ashbury district of San Francisco had spread south and was being marketed by evangelical entrepreneurs like Duane Pederson, a former gospel magician turned publisher of the "Hollywood Free Paper"; Arthur Blessitt, an evangelist who became known as the Pastor of Sunset Strip (and who also set a world record for pulling a cross on wheels across the United

States); and Pat Boone, a former pop singer who was performing mass baptisms in the Pacific Ocean.

The Jesus Movement, like most of the youth movements of the 1960s, had a revolutionary, anti-institutional feel to it. Traditional denominational churches ("the establishment") were slow to respond to this new religious fervor and looked at most of what was going on with suspicion, if not outright contempt. As a result, many new youth churches were formed, some of them arising out of communes and coffeehouses. Chuck Smith's Calvary Chapel in Costa Mesa was one of the more prominent of these and later became a denomination of its own.

But most of us who were doing youth ministry at that time were just trying to take advantage of what appeared to be a genuine youth revival. Our youth group at First Nazarene Church had grown from thirty or so raised-in-the-church kids to more than a hundred teenagers, many of them brand new Christians. I did my best to introduce these new converts to the culture and customs of our particular denomination, but their presence in our worship services and even the hallways of our church made everyone uncomfortable. These "street kids" didn't know how to behave in church, and they dressed inappropriately. They had long hair, and word had somehow leaked that one or more of the kids were known pot smokers.

Not only were the adults of the church uncomfortable, but the youth were uncomfortable too. They were getting a strong message from the church leadership that their salvation and good standing with the church had more to do with their dress and behavior than the finished work of Christ on the cross and the grace and mercy of God.

So I got the boot in 1971. I think most of the kids in the youth group left the church about the same time.

After my experience at First Nazarene I grew a bit disillusioned with the institutional church and wasn't sure I wanted to return to one. So I didn't go looking for another church position right away. My wife and I opened up our rented house in East San Diego for a weekly Bible study, which became a safe haven for many of my former students, plus neighbors who were also feeling somewhat disenfranchised by the church. For about two years our living room was packed with young people every Wednesday night to listen to John MacArthur tapes and to pray. While we didn't call it a church, it certainly felt like one to us.

John MacArthur had been one of the most popular speakers at our junior high camps at Forest Home and other youth events around Southern California. We were pretty good friends and had on several occasions appeared at youth events around Southern California together—John would speak and the Rice Kryspies would perform. When John began pastoring his father's former church, Grace Community Church in Panorama City, he was one of the first I know to make his sermons available to church members on cassettes, a brand-new technology in the early 1970s. Many young people who were coming to Christ in the Jesus Movement were listening to John MacArthur tapes.

MacArthur was an expository preacher—verse-by-verse teaching on various books of the Bible. His sermons were relatively long at around sixty minutes each, but our Bible study group loved listening to those tapes. On occasion, we invited him to our home to take questions from our group, and he was always willing to come.

Most people would be rather surprised to know that Youth Specialties began marketing John MacArthur tapes around that time. We called them "Cassette Bible Studies" and they were featured in the first Youth Specialties catalog, right there alongside our *Ideas* books and a line of very embarrassing Christian bumper stickers ("Honk if you love Jesus"). After a few months we discontinued the bumper stickers. Around the same time Rev. MacArthur discontinued his relationship with us. He wasn't the first to get upset over a magazine that we started publishing in June of 1971.

THE DOOR

Mike and I were fans of a feisty little newsletter published by two good friends of ours, Paul Sailhamer and Gary Wilburn, called *The Wittenburg Door*. Paul and Gary—just like Mike and me—were former YFC guys who had transitioned to church ministry and found much of the culture of the church seriously in need of change. The newsletter was named after the famous door in Wittenberg, Germany, where Martin Luther nailed ninety-five theses which triggered the Protestant Reformation. Mimeographed on two sheets of paper and stapled together, *The Wittenburg Door* had the motto "There is no public reform that was not first a private opinion." It contained some very funny as well as thought-provoking articles on evangelicalism, youth ministry and the church. When they ran out of money to keep their newsletter in print, they decided to discontinue their fledgling publishing venture.

Mike and I loved the satirical bent to *The Wittenburg Door*, as both of us had grown up reading *Mad* magazine and were well acquainted with what a powerful medium humor could be for communicating controversial ideas. Both of us had written for underground student newspapers, which were also the rage at that time. So we approached Paul and Gary about the possibility of taking over their newsletter and publishing it in a magazine format, and they were more than happy to give it to us.[1]

With my new degree in graphic design in hand, I went to work immediately on a design for the masthead of the magazine.

Neither of us knew anything about editing a magazine, so we asked our friend Ben Patterson if he would be willing to do it. Ben had worked with us at Forest Home, and while he had no prior magazine experience, we knew he was a very good writer. He agreed to do it and we published our first issue of the *Wittenburg Door* in June of 1971.

After our first issue was published, I discovered that I had misspelled *Wittenberg* on the front cover of the magazine. Several of our readers pointed out the mistake, and we courageously came up with explanation that we chose the name *Wittenburg* just to be unique—which of course was a lie.

The original aim of the magazine was to be a voice for youth ministry in the church. But unlike later magazines—such as our own *Youthworker* journal or *Group* magazine—which carried articles about youth ministry philosophy and practice, we wanted to change the church and *make the case* for youth ministry. Our protest was that the church for too long had ignored young people. We wanted to stimulate discussion on that issue and bring about some real change. Our first issue had Hal Lindsey on the cover. A former Campus Crusade staff worker at UCLA who started a new youth ministry in Hollywood called the Jesus Christ Light and Power Company, he had also just written a bestselling book called *The Late Great Planet Earth*. In the interview Hal said, "I think that what we're seeing is a switch-over from what it's been in the past with its traditions to a new face, a new form of the church. . . . Kids hate anything that is impersonal, highly organized, highly structured, large and irrelevant. And I've just given you a description of the average church."[2]

Interestingly enough, that quote could easily be mistaken for a quote from any one of numerous books or blogs on youth ministry today. While we didn't agree with everything Hal Lindsey had to say, we definitely agreed with him on his appraisal of the church, and we were on a quest to do something about it. The inaugural issue of *The Door* (as it came to be called) also carried an editorial by Ben on the death of the Jesus Movement, and Mike wrote a piece called "Another Diary of a Mad Housewife," a fictional but powerful story of a youth worker's wife who was fed up with her workaholic husband. I wrote an article called "The Progress Game" comparing stupid things youth workers did in the 1950s with stupid things currently being done. We also started a monthly feature called "Profile of a Youth Group" highlighting church youth ministries around the country we thought were unique and newsworthy.

Mike was always fond of Ernest Hemingway's idea that good writers should have a "built-in, shock-proof crap detector"[3] so part of our mission included pointing out the speck in everybody else's eye. We started a column called "Loser of the Month" (with its famous Green Weenie award) and another called "Truth Is Stranger Than Fiction," which featured outrageous examples of (mostly) evangelical absurdities.

But in the early going we were angry young youth workers pushing the church to start taking youth ministry more seriously. In one early issue, we took a cheap shot at *Christianity Today* magazine because they ran an editorial piece which included this quotation:

> The accent on youth is one of the clichés of our day. It always has to be the same kind of thing: their great intelligence, their honesty, their opinions which always must be listened to. . . . If you are a Bible-believing Christian, you might want to look in the Bible for a youth program. I search in vain. The accent on youth is nowhere in Holy Writ.[4]

We didn't provide any reference at all for that quote—which issue it was in, who wrote it or why. We just quoted it and did a little editorializing ourselves, accusing them of having their collective heads in the sand. "Thank you *Christianity Today* for pointing out that the Bible is an *adult* book and for reminding us that the answer for our so-called youth problems is for adults to 'train them in their homes.'"[5]

I don't remember who wrote that editorial, but if I did, I suppose an apology is in order. But what we heard the editors at *Christianity Today* saying back then was that youth ministry is unbiblical and therefore unjustified. We took this as a shot across the bow of our calling from a respected evangelical voice. My guess is that it was not so much an attack on youth ministry as it was a warning meant to help prevent the kind of mistakes we are all now trying to correct.

THINKING ABOUT THE CHURCH

It seems like we've been trying to make the church a safe place for teenagers for a long time.

Back in my YFC days, I tried to do "follow up" on teenagers who had made decisions to receive Christ. Part of that process was to help these young believers get plugged into a local church. But few churches in those days knew what to do with young people who arrived on their doorsteps with a newfound faith and a lot of questions that didn't have easy answers. Many of these kids with their long hair and hippie clothes were looked upon with suspicion if not outright contempt, and they were more often than not required to clean up and conform to the prevailing church culture before they would ever feel welcome.

Besides the "smoking gun" of Mike's controversial talk, one of the issues which led to my dismissal at the Nazarene Church was the insistence that I enforce a dress code for the teens of the church, which included slacks for the boys and modest dresses for the girls. Apparently some of the older members of the church were upset with the blue jeans and short skirts (remember hot pants?) that some of our teens were wearing to church on Sunday mornings. My argument to them that *we should at least be happy they are coming* seemed to fall on deaf ears.

We've come a long way. Most churches today have full-time youth pastors and provide a variety of relevant programs for young people. Some have multiple youth staffs and multiple youth groups—for middle-schoolers, high school students, college students and various other affinity groups as well. Many churches have made significant financial commitments to youth ministry by erecting impressive buildings where youth groups can conduct their own worship services, outreach events and function pretty much as churches within churches.

But is this what we really had in mind? Have our youth ministries successfully provided the bridge for helping teenagers make their transition into adulthood with their faith intact?[6] In his book *They Like Jesus but Not the Church*, Dan Kimball lists some of the reasons why so many young people today are turned off by the church. In his view, emerging generations believe that the church is an organized religion with a political agenda, judgmental and negative, dominated by males and oppressing females, homophobic, arrogant, judgmental and fundamentalist.[7] Kimball provides plenty of good examples to illustrate his points, but as I was reading his book, the thought crossed my mind more than once that I don't think the young people Kimball describes have ever actually been part of a real church. Maybe they have been part of a youth group and maybe they have actually attended a few church services, but have they ever been part of an actual church?

I don't deny that many youth are justified in their negative view of the church, but I think we all have a tendency to hold negative views of people and organizations we know little or nothing about. There is a fast food chain which I absolutely refuse to visit because twenty years ago I ate a taco there which made me very sick. I'm sure this particular restaurant chain has improved since then, and I may go there again someday if I'm really hungry and have no other choice, but for now I'm comfortable holding on to my completely irrational belief that this particular fast food chain (which rhymes with Sack in the Fox) is out to kill me.

When I hear some young people complain about the church I often wonder if maybe we didn't somehow give them a bad taco. When youth groups function as alternatives to the church rather than a vital part of it, teenagers don't experience what the church has to offer them. Even though they have fond memories of the activities and fun things they did while in the youth group, they feel no real connection to the church nor do they have an understanding of its traditions and values, which aren't readily apparent. As they go on with their young adult lives, they choose to believe the negative stereotypes of the church which are promoted heavily in the world in which they live.

> What we have today is not really a youth ministry problem. It's a church problem. Truth is—it has *always* been a church problem.

All kinds of innovative youth ministry models are being proposed these days by people who are much better qualified than me to reinvent youth ministry. But what we have today is not really a youth ministry problem. It's a church problem. Truth is—it has *always* been a church problem. When the baby boomer generation forced the church to take young people seriously, it did so by hiring youth workers to warehouse them and keep them busy with fun and games and other programs especially for teenagers. Now several generations later we are seeing the result of all that. It's easy to point fingers at everyone responsible for keeping a defective model of youth ministry in place for so long, but changing how we do youth ministry, or even abolishing it altogether, won't stem the tide of young people leaving the church and their faith as they get older. We really need to change how we do church.

Over the years I've watched youth workers leave YS conventions or other youth ministry training events after being challenged to work more with parents or to recruit more volunteers or to become more missional, only to return to churches that don't want them to change a thing and wouldn't support them if they did. They go home with a whole new vision and a backpack full of ideas only to fail at the implementation stage. They learn very quickly that unless some fundamental changes are made on the church level, there really won't be much chance of any lasting change on the youth ministry level. It's a little bit like putting a brand new set of tires on a car without an engine. You really aren't going to get very far.

Most youth pastors feel pretty frustrated when I say that they probably aren't going to be able to change things in their youth ministry unless the church changes too. They know I'm calling for something that is impossible to do. It's not the job of a youth pastor to change the church. In fact if they try to change the church, they find themselves looking for a new one real quick.

That's true. But we all know that churches don't change overnight and there never will be a perfect church—at least not until Jesus returns. Some might call it the tail wagging the dog, but I believe that youth ministry—just because of it's risk-taking, entrepreneurial nature—is capable of pushing the envelope and bringing about real change in the church over time. I've seen it happen already. Remember, there was a time when the vast majority of churches did nothing at all to respond to the needs of the emerging youth culture. When you look at where the church is today compared with where it was just a few decades ago, a tremendous amount of change has indeed taken place.

Real and lasting change inevitably happens that way, gradually and slowly. I think it's profoundly sad that so many young leaders elect not to wait for the church to change but instead to start new churches which bear little resemblance to the churches of their parents and grandparents. Some of the popular church leadership conferences targeting "church leaders under the age of forty" remind me of the mistakes we made in the early days of youth ministry when we arrogantly thought we had all the answers and rolled our eyes at older generations who urged caution. Maybe letting traditional churches die and starting over with new improved churches catering to emerging generations is the right thing do to—only time will tell—but I have a feeling that many of these new churches will experience the same kind of generational disconnect and discomfort that traditional churches have experienced before them, and the cycle will likely be repeated again and again.

Kimball points out that the great cathedrals and church buildings of Europe, once filled with people, now sit empty on Sunday mornings. "We shouldn't think that we're above such a thing happening here," he writes.

> With the increasing drop-out rate of people in emerging generations, it could be our destiny that in thirty or forty years, all of our recently constructed megachurch buildings which are now filled with people, will end up as virtually empty tourist attractions.[8]

That will only happen if we allow it to happen. This may seem like a tall order, changing the church. But it can be done. In the early days of youth ministry, the church was changed one church at a time. As a few local churches began hiring youth directors and youth pastors, others followed suit, and within a few years monumental changes had taken place over the entire youth ministry landscape. Arguments can be made about whether those changes were positive or negative, but there's no question that the church has gone through some significant changes. And it can change again.

DO WE NEED YOUTH MINISTRY?

Perhaps the first step in changing the church is to challenge the assumption that every church needs a professional youth ministry staff. Do we really need a youth ministry in order to raise up children who, like Jesus, grow "in wisdom and strength and in favor with God and man" (Luke 2:52)? That's what parents want for their kids, and that's also what we want to see happen in the lives of each one of the kids in our youth ministries. So the question we really should be asking is: what will encourage that kind of healthy growth and maturity in our young people? Does that really require a youth pastor?

Many churches are afraid to ask those questions. Or they don't bother because (1) "We've always had a youth pastor," (2) "We want to reach teenagers, and we can't do that without a youth pastor," (3) "Our senior pastor doesn't have the time for youth ministry," (4) "We don't have any volunteers who are qualified or willing to do it," (5) "Every other church in town has a youth pastor," (6) "Families with teenagers won't come unless we have a youth pastor," (7) "It's already in the church budget" and so on. So a youth pastor stays until something bad happens and is let go, or he feels the call of God to a bigger church, or she decides it's time to go back to school, or just simply quits and leaves the church looking for a replacement. The youth ministry implodes and the students are left traumatized, damaging their relationship with God and the church. The church quickly hires a replacement youth pastor who may or may not be able to connect with the students left behind by the old one, and this cycle repeats itself over and over again.

A thirteen-year-old boy named Austin recently told me, "This has been a very bad year for me. My parents got a divorce and my church got a new youth pastor." I'm not sure which of these events he considered worse—but clearly the loss of his former youth pastor ranked high as a significant crisis in his life.

As we discussed in the last chapter, all this is the natural result of the professionalizing of youth ministry, plus our insatiable appetite for outsourcing almost everything we don't have time to do ourselves. As we get busier and busier, we look for other people who, for a reasonable price will mow our lawns, clean our houses, do our shopping and help raise our kids. Parents not only outsource the spiritual training of their kids to the church, but the church outsources it to a professional youth pastor.

There is a church in Southern California which recently had to let their youth pastor go because of economic difficulties. Rather than hiring a new one, the church decided to go back to an all-volunteer youth ministry. But this very large church— with hundreds of adult members—ended up having to *cancel* almost all of the youth ministry programs because they couldn't find any volunteers to lead them. They couldn't go back to a volunteer-driven youth ministry because the congregation had been trained for too many years to believe that youth ministry was just not their job.

Youth pastors can serve a much needed and very important role in the church, as we discussed in the last chapter. But no church should ever hire a youth pastor and then turn the youth ministry entirely over to him or to her. Youth ministry is too important for youth pastors. I don't mean any disrespect by saying that; the spiritual formation of children and youth is the responsibility of not just the youth pastor but the entire congregation.

VISION AND MISSION

I know that senior pastors usually have their plates full, but the vision and mission for youth ministry in a local church must come from the top. According to researchers at Search Institute,

> The senior pastor of a local church will likely have more influence and power over the youth ministry than a youth pastor. Besides the fact that senior pastors generally have more control over the vision and climate of the church than youth pastors, studies consistently show that senior pastor rank higher than youth pastors with students when it comes to spiritual influence and long-lasting impact in their lives.[9]

I'm not suggesting that youth pastors don't have any influence or that they should become senior pastors in order to have a lasting influence on youth; I'm only saying that the youth pastor is there to implement the vision and mission for youth ministry that has been adopted by the entire congregation. The common practice of hiring youth pastors who bring their own vision of youth ministry to the church more often than not results in disaster. In most cases, hired guns from the outside have no history with the church or the youth who are part of it. In some cases, they bring with them a philosophy of ministry or even a theology which is counter to the ministry goals and theology of the local church.

Youth ministry is too important for youth pastors.

Many churches have had success hiring from within. Some of the most effective youth workers I've known have emerged from within the churches they were serving. They may have grown up in the youth ministry themselves or were older adults who felt called to ministry later on in life. I visited a church recently where a businessman in the church sold his chain of flower shops and became the youth pastor—and a very good one at that. Because he had been a member of that church for many years he was already well liked and had a great appreciation for the history and unique climate of the church. His experience as a businessman in the local community gave him relationships and connections that gave him a tremendous advantage as a leader of both youth and adults in the church.

Whether the youth pastor comes from within or without, the vision and mission of the youth ministry must be in harmony with that of the local church. There are plenty of wonderful youth ministry philosophies to choose from these days, but they should not be adopted unless they match up well with the vision and mission of the local church. For example, there's a trend today toward teaching students ancient spiritual practices such as meditation, prayer walks, labyrinths, chanting the Jesus prayer, making the sign of the cross, praying with icons and so on. I have no problem with any of these; I practice some of them myself. But unless they are encouraged and a familiar part of local church's tradition, they are likely to be nothing more than gimmicks and of no more value than any other mountaintop experience that we typically give teenagers. Unique and memorable spiritual experiences are good things but our kids need to know that they can also be had in the regular rhythm of their normal churchgoing experience, no matter how commonplace and predictable it may be. Young people need to learn how to worship, how to serve and how to be in fellowship with other members of the local congregation. Later on, when they feel a need to draw close to God, they may not be able to find a labyrinth but they'll surely be able to find their church.

I'm not discounting the value of ancient forms of spiritual discipline and worship, nor am I opposed to mountaintop experiences. I've had quite a few of them. They are unique and memorable, but they don't happen frequently, and they are never required for me to know that Jesus is Lord and that God is near. I've learned to be content with knowing that I can have an experience with God every time I sit in church on Sunday morning and sing the hymns, recite the creeds, hear the good news proclaimed and look into the faces of those who sit in the pews next to me. Teenagers need to learn the same contentment if we hope for them to be sustained in their faith into adulthood.

THE SIREN CALL OF MUSIC

For about two years, Marci and I continued hosting our neighborhood Bible study which served as our church. I worked full time for Youth Specialties at our downtown office and also played in a weekend country band called Brush Arbor, formed in 1972 when the Rice Kryspies (my family band) merged with another group from Los Angeles called Kentucky Faith.

The Jesus Movement had created a huge demand for Christian bands to play the coffee houses and concerts that were springing up all over the place. Our style was country-rock, a cross between the Byrds and Buck Owens. We tried to get signed by a record label but none of the Christian labels (all two of them) were interested in us, because we insisted on playing secular music as well as songs with a Christian message. As it turned out, we were signed by Capitol Records and ended up with a couple of top ten country singles and a few appearances on the Grand Ole Opry in Nashville. We also got to do a short tour with Johnny Cash and appear with him on his NBC-TV show.

But we still performed at churches and other venues around Southern California. I remember a concert we did at Calvary Chapel in Costa Mesa with Love Song, the Second Chapter of Acts and several other popular Christian bands. Many of those artists had left *worldly music* to play *Jesus music,* and they couldn't understand why we hadn't done the same. They actually held a prayer meeting backstage on our behalf. We appreciated their concern for us, but our view at the time was that any song could be a Christian song if a Christian sang it. Besides, we didn't want to be known as a Christian band who was *country.* We wanted to be known as a country band who was *Christian.* There's a big difference.

After Brush Arbor won Best Vocal Group at the 1974 Academy of Country Music Awards, our booking agent told us he would keep us on the road three hundred days a year. I knew I couldn't keep playing music and working at Youth Specialties. God had called me youth ministry, not to country music. Besides, my son was turning two years old, and I couldn't be away from home three hundred days a year. So Brush Arbor turned out to be a very memorable excursion into the world of country music which ended for me early in 1974.[10] For the next twenty years I was fully engaged in the mission of Youth Specialties.

After I quit Brush Arbor, Marci and I started looking for a real church. We had moved to a new neighborhood, so our Bible study group no longer met in our home. Like most parents who grew up in church—no matter how old-fashioned the church of their childhood might have been—we wanted our children to have a similar church experience growing up.

We heard about a new church called Morning Star Lutheran that had recently started up in a rented building not far from our house, so we decided to check it out. Neither my wife nor I had ever attended a Lutheran church before, so we had no idea what to expect. We were completely lost that first Sunday as we fumbled through what seemed like a very confusing order of worship. It seemed more like a Catholic mass than any kind of church service I had ever attended. I really didn't know what to make of it all. But two things really hooked me at that first service.

The first was how they did communion, or what they called "the celebration of the Eucharist." It was a far cry from what I was used to, with little plastic cups, styrofoam wafers and fifteen verses of "There Is a Fountain Filled with Blood." It was obvious that a solemn and holy ritual was being performed here, with various chants and motions and everyone knowing exactly what to say and do at the appropriate times. The pastor wore a robe with colorful vestments, and he grinned broadly as he broke the bread (a whole loaf of it), proclaimed it "the body of Christ, broken for you!" and allowed each one of us to take a small portion. Then he lifted the cup, blessed it in the same way and brought it around to each of us to either take a sip or dip our bread in the cup. It wasn't grape juice as I expected but real wine. I almost choked but was definitely thinking, *Now this is a very cool church.*

Then the clincher. The pastor brought out his banjo and started to play a folk hymn. Now I actually *did* choke. He wasn't a particularly great banjo player, but given my taste in music, I suddenly knew that I had found my church. Yee-haw!

We kept going back and eventually became members. For almost eight years, I served as the youth pastor at Morning Star Church in an unofficial way. Since I was making my living from selling *Ideas* books, the church didn't have to put me on the payroll. At the time there were seven teenagers in the youth group and I came to know and love each one of them and their families very well. The youth group grew however, topping out at around thirty kids after a few years. I recruited several other adult leaders and parents who helped share the load of teaching, counseling and activity planning. We usually had one weekly youth group meeting at my home and a Sunday school class which met at the church before the worship service. We also did most of the activities most youth groups of that era did—lock-ins, camping trips, fundraisers, mission trips. It was during this time that I wrote a couple of Youth Specialties books called *Great Ideas for Small Youth Groups* and *Up Close and Personal*, a book on how to build community.

What I remember most about that youth group is that even though we had youth group functions, there was never a time when those students ever felt that they weren't vitally connected to the rest of the church. Attending the regular adult worship service on Sunday morning was simply a non-negotiable part of being Lutheran. As I discovered, pretty much all Lutheran churches conduct their services more or less the same way (with perhaps the exception of our banjo-playing pastor) and with little debate over worship style preferences or sermon topics. Every Sunday the same gospel was proclaimed, the same creeds recited and the same sacraments celebrated.

I remember being incredibly bored by some of these very traditional Lutheran services, and embarrassed by some amateurish and awkward moments in others, but I don't remember the teenagers ever resisting or refusing to attend because they weren't entertaining or cool. I only mention this because I find that many kids today (even in Lutheran churches) have been conditioned to be less tolerant of worship experiences which aren't very entertaining.

After the banjo-playing pastor left Morning Star and the new chain-smoking one tried to turn me into a genuine card-carrying Lutheran (I held out on a few doctrinal issues), Marci and I departed to help plant a new church in El Cajon. Community Covenant Church was part of the Evangelical Covenant denomination. Our core group of founders included several youth workers, some of whom were colleagues of mine at Youth Specialties. We chose the name of the church based on our desire to create a community of believers much like the one described in Acts 2:42-47. We wanted our new church to be like the early church, having all things in common, sharing their possessions with each other, eating together and worshiping together as one body in Christ.

Part of our vision included not forming a youth group. Never mind that we had no youth at the time to populate a youth group (lots of young families) but we really did want to make *the church itself* the youth group—inclusive of all ages. Rather than having youth retreats, we would have all-church retreats. Rather than having youth mission trips, we would have all-church mission trips. Rather than planning social events for the youth, we would have social events for the whole church. Rather than a youth worship service, we would design our regular worship services mindful of all the generations in attendance. We just figured that if kids weren't connecting with what was happening in the adult service, there was a strong likelihood that nobody else was connecting with it either. Sure, there would be times when the kids met up separately from the adults for age-specific teaching times and fun activities, but our goal was for the youth to feel part of the adult community and fully accepted as full-fledged members of the church.

That's pretty much how we did church there at Community Covenant for ten years or so. My wife and I chose to leave that church after I left Youth Specialties in 1994, and it has since grown in numbers and taken a bit more conventional approach to youth ministry. It's still a great church, not perfect by any stretch, but we loved raising our children there. When our daughter Amber was about thirteen years old, my wife overheard a conversation she had with one of her friends from school. "My church is so huuuuge!" said her friend, bragging about the megachurch she attended across town. "And our youth pastor is awesome! He plays in a band and knows all kinds of famous people. Our youth group meets in the new gym and it's really fun! We're going to winter camp in a few weeks and later on we're going to Disneyland and Magic Mountain!"

"Well . . ." said Amber, "my church loves me."

7

THE EXPANSION OF YOUTH MINISTRY
Thinking About the Future

"Who's on first, what's on second, I don't know is on third base!"

Those lines are forever etched in my brain. They're from one of Mike Yaconelli's favorite comedy routines, "Who's on First?" by Abbott and Costello. Mike had the Lou Costello part down pat and he insisted that I memorize Bud Abbott's half of the dialogue. We performed it whenever we had the chance, but I rarely got through that skit without cracking up at Mike. He really got into it. "Third base!" he would yell, as his eyes got big, and I'd start laughing right along with the audience.

We published the script to "Who's on First?" in one of our early *Ideas* books, only to get a very stern cease-and-desist letter from a lawyer representing the Abbott and Costello estate. That wouldn't be the last letter we got from lawyers before we learned the legalities of the publishing business.

I played straight man to Mike for quite a few years. In fact, our names became indelibly linked because of all the Rice and Yaconelli books that were coming out during the 1970s—especially the *Ideas* books. We started getting a few speaking invitations around the country, and one of the first was in Kansas

City in the spring of 1970. We were amazed when more than a hundred people showed up to hear us talk about youth ministry and demonstrate ideas from our books.

A few months later we took another speaking engagement at a church convention being held at an ultraconservative Baptist college in Springfield, Missouri. Apparently the person who invited us had never seen a picture of either one of us because when he met us at the airport, he seemed to go into shock. He went to a pay phone there in the airport, made a call and informed us that our speaking engagement would have to be cancelled. "No long hair or beards are allowed on the campus," he said. "And you can't wear bell bottoms."

We didn't mind being discriminated against because of our hair, but we definitely took offense when he insulted our snappy bell-bottom pants. Being the rebels we were, we decided not to go to a barber shop or buy new clothes. We were stuck in Springfield anyway and our not-very-gracious hosts made it clear they weren't going to cover our travel expenses. So we made arrangements with a hotel near the college to use one of their conference rooms for a seminar the next evening. With a felt-tip pen, I sketched out a one page flyer advertising a "Youth Programming Seminar with Rice and Yaconelli" which we got printed at a local Postal Instant Press. Armed with several hundred flyers, we hit that Baptist convention with a full frontal assault, plastering those flyers all over the campus until several security men escorted us off the premises, doing their best to confiscate all the flyers we were scattering up and down the corridors.

We really didn't think anyone at all would show up for that seminar, but somehow the word got around and nearly a hundred youth workers had the courage to defy church leaders and come off campus for a youth ministry seminar. It went great, and we sold all the *Ideas* books we brought with us.

It wasn't long before Mike and I started conducting our own one-day "youth programming seminars" in a few cities around the country and then later renamed it the National Resource Seminar for Youth Workers. The first year we did four cities, then twelve cities, then thirty-five cities, and eventually (after we expanded our seminar team) we took it to more than a hundred cities. Mike and I, along with Denny Rydberg, did most of the teaching during the 1970s, but as we grew, we added a top notch team of presenters including Jim Burns, Bill McNabb, Ray Johnston, Rich Van Pelt, Les Christie, Duffy Robbins and several other youth worker friends of ours.

We did a lot of advertising in the early years, primarily with direct mail. Our early promotional materials were always done with a sense of humor. Mike was great at writing hilarious copy for completely ridiculous cover letters which in most cases made fun of direct mail advertising. Some of our mailings even had "Junk Mail Department" printed right on the envelope next to our return address. One year the National Direct Marketing Association was so offended by what we were doing that they gave us the award for "worst direct mail marketer of the year." But our mailings actually quadrupled the national average for direct mail response, so we got the last laugh.

Every year we promoted our National Resource Seminar for Youth Workers with a different theme, which had us dressed up as baseball players, construction workers, safari guides, orchestra members, gas station attendants or some other goofy costumes. Our intentionally ridiculous attempts to tie those themes in with youth ministry were just crazy enough keep people coming to our seminars year after year. One year we dressed up as chefs using the tagline "We're Cooking Up Some Great Youth Ministry Ideas." That same year Mike and I were invited to conduct youth ministry seminars on military bases in West Germany (there were still two Germanys back then). To promote our seminar in Frankfurt, our hosts put the picture of the two of us in chef hats on a poster with the caption "Rice and Yaconelli Are Cooking Up Some Great Ideas!" Apparently something got lost in the translation, and about three hundred people showed up for that seminar expecting a cooking demonstration and a free meal. We sent out for some Kentucky Fried Chicken and did our best to keep the crowd entertained with some music, fun and games until the food showed up; we even resorted to another performance of "Who's on First?"

Despite our lack of business acumen, Youth Specialties continued to grow. Fortunately we were always blessed with someone who was much better organized than either one of us and able to referee our frequent disagreements. Denny Rydberg was that guy for about ten years. He departed in 1981 to work with Campus Crusade for Christ and then a church in Seattle, and eventually ended up as president of Young Life. Taking Denny's place at Youth Specialties was a talented and personable twenty-five-year-old named Ronald "Tic" Long, who ran our office and managed most of our events. Tic later served as president of Youth Specialties for several years and was a tremendous asset to our company.

Rice and Yaconelli Are Cooking Up Some Great Ideas!

We grew fast during the 1970s and 1980s, and so did the entire youth ministry industry. While evangelical churches were our initial and primary market, many mainline protestant and Catholic churches began hiring full-time youth workers and sending them to our events. Mike and I commissioned a rewrite of our entire *Ideas* library for Catholic publisher St. Mary's Press, and many of those books continue to be sold to this day.

The demand for youth ministry training and resources seemed limitless. We launched a branch of Youth Specialties in Australia and traveled to New Zealand, Great Britain, Europe and Latin America to help train youth workers in those countries. As other youth ministry organizations and ministries emerged during the 1970s, like Group Publishing, Sonlife, the National Network of Youth Ministries, Reach Out Ministries and others, we knew that youth workers were being confronted with a lot more choices. So part of our business plan at Youth Specialties was to leverage the growth of the industry by bringing everyone together at our National Youth Workers Conventions and to use our one-day seminars around the country to showcase not only what we were doing but what everyone else was doing as well. For several years in the early 1980s we published an annual *National Resource Directory for Youth Workers,* something of a youth ministry yellow pages. Whether it was true or not, we wanted to at least give the impression that we weren't in competition with anybody who was trying to advance the cause of effective youth ministry.

We were willing to take risks in the early days and I think that's a big reason why so many youth workers were willing to trust us as leaders rather than keepers of the status quo. Of course, our unwillingness to play it safe also got us into a lot of trouble at times and invited a lot of criticism. But I think many youth workers came to our conventions year after year just to find out what was new, where things were going. I can still remember the shock waves that went through the room in 1981 when the punk band Undercover hit the stage for the first time with their bleached Mohawk hairdos, tattoos, chains and torn denim jeans shouting "God rules!" over a violent flurry of drum and guitar solos that made walls shake and ears bleed. Our goal was never to offend anyone but rather to present the broad spectrum of youth ministry trends and ideas. At the conclusion of our conventions we always made the effort to bring everyone together for a celebration of our unity in Christ, usually with a nondenominational communion service.

When Mike and I parted company in 1994, I don't think either one of us had any idea what the future of Youth Specialties would look like. I don't think either one of us could have predicted the incredible growth that youth ministry (and Youth Specialties) experienced during the 1990s. After I left YS, I attended most of the National Youth Workers Conventions, sometimes as a seminar leader but mostly as an exhibitor (plugging my Understanding Your Teenager seminars) and was always amazed by the sheer numbers of people who were coming. The events were held not in hotel ballrooms but in huge convention centers and arenas. The main sessions of the convention had become major theatrical productions, a far cry from the days when I would stand on a small stage with guitar in hand, leading a few hundred people in the latest batch of fun songs and praise choruses. I can't tell you how many people (mostly old timers) would spot me in the crowd and ask, "Did you and Mike ever imagine that Youth Specialties would get this big?" And of course the answer was no. We simply rode a wave that had become something of a tsunami.

THE EXPANSION OF YOUTH MINISTRY

Where is youth ministry headed now? Will it continue to thrive and expand at the same pace it has over the past forty years? Is youth ministry still a growth industry? Only time will tell, of course, but there are clear signs that the youth ministry landscape has changed dramatically and will continue to do so in the years to come. I think it's safe to say that no single organization or leader (Youth Specialties or anyone else) will be able to chart the course or set the agenda for what youth ministry will look like in the future.

I was at a church youth group meeting recently and I couldn't help but notice that while the young musicians on stage were earnestly trying to lead the group in the latest lineup of contemporary worship songs, it was pretty clear that only about 30 percent of the students were connecting with what was going on in any meaningful or visible way. This is fairly typical of most youth groups today. When I compare that to the days when we could have 95 percent of the group singing along and doing the hand motions to "Pharoah Pharoah" with uninhibited enthusiasm, it's obvious that things have changed in a big way.

Many years ago I was listening to an "oldies" station on the radio and my daughter Amber said, "You know, dad, my generation won't have any oldies." As I thought more about her comment, I realized she was right. The monolithic one-size-fits-all youth culture of the past has been replaced by a tribalistic choose-your-own-adventure assortment of youth subcultures. For that reason alone, there is no longer one approach to youth ministry programming that could ever possibly meet the needs of all teenagers. I could list here a sampling of the many youth subcultures that you will find on a typical middle school or high school campus these days, but there wouldn't be room to list them all, and I'm sure the list would be outdated by the time this book was published. There are literally hundreds of youth microcultures which now exist simply because of the increased ability for teens to be more selective about the kinds of music and lifestyles they choose to consume or identify themselves with.

Youth ministry of the past fifty years has been built on the dirty little secret that only white suburban churches could afford to hire youth pastors and provide them with the money to go to the conventions and buy all the resources. In the early 1990s I remember proposing to our publishers a book on urban youth ministry; it was rejected simply because after assessing the market for such a book, it was clear that it would lose money. I understand how the publishing business works, but I always regretted that we couldn't do more at Youth Specialties to help nonwhite churches with their youth ministries. We offered a few elective seminars for urban youth workers at our National Youth Workers Conventions but they were never very well attended. Few nonwhite youth workers were inclined to attend a convention with so many white faces on the program.

When Bart Campolo approached us in the early 1990s to help him organize a convention in Philadelphia for urban youth workers, I wanted very badly for us to do it, but it just never penciled out as a worthwhile venture. Bart went ahead with his convention anyway and for several years his Kingdomworks conferences made a significant contribution to the advancement of urban, nonwhite youth ministry. Since then Youth Specialties as well as many other youth ministry organizations have made great strides to address the changing demographics of the adolescent population, but youth ministry of the future will have to change if for no other reason than to address the changing ethnicity of the adolescent population.

I asked a youth pastor friend of mine how many students normally attend his youth group and he answered "Fifty—five at a time." The sum total of all kinds of small groups with different kinds of kids in different locations comprised his youth group. They rarely ever met together in the same place at the same time. Mark Oestreicher, former president of Youth Specialties, suggests in his book *Youth Ministry 3.0* breaking ministries down into smaller, separate youth groups, each targeting one of the various youth subcultures that exist in our local communities. Since one youth ministry will only reach one kind of kid, he reasons, multiple youth ministries within the same church have the opportunity to reach youth "in multiple youth culture contexts."[1] I've advocated something along these same lines myself in the past; if our youth ministry model remains an attractional one—as it has been for more than fifty years—then the division of our youth groups into smaller affinity groups makes perfect sense. It's probably the only way to reach out to youth who have not yet become integrated into the church. It seems to me that this is essentially an adaptation of the parachurch model of youth ministry to the postmodern realities of today's youth culture.

But while the subdivision of youth ministry into smaller affinity groups seems like a logical solution to the postmodern challenges of individualism and diversity, I've had reservations about this approach for some time because I think it's based on a flawed view of the church. I'm still holding out for a model of youth ministry that offers teenagers something very different from the world in which they live—a place where every affinity group lays aside their differences to find their unity in Christ.

When local churches adopted the parachurch model of youth ministry in the 1960s and 1970s, most of the established parachurch ministries began scrambling to justify their existence. Some had to reinvent themselves or dissolve entirely. Churches that previously supported YFC and Young Life with people and financial support began reallocating their resources to fund

their own youth ministry programs. Most parachurch ministries today find it very tough to survive in today's economy, but
they're important: we should be sending missionaries to reach
kids on their turf just as we have done in the past and which
many still do so well today. There are millions of teenagers who
still need to hear the good news about Jesus, and they are not
likely to ever darken the doors of our churches until they do.

There's nothing wrong with the parachurch model of doing
youth ministry. It's just not the model that is appropriate for a
local church. For the church, I keep returning to the kind of
youth ministry that was invented by Moses. In my opinion,
Moses should go down as the first youth worker in history. In
fact, he published the first youth ministry idea book and it had
some pretty good stuff in it:

- Impress these things on your children.

- Talk about them when you sit at home.

- Talk about them while you walk along the road.

- Talk about them at bedtime.

- Talk about them when you get up in the morning.

- Tie them as symbols on your hands.

- Bind them on your foreheads.

- Nail them to the doorposts of your houses.

- Write them on your front gates.

- Do the egg-and-armpit relay.

Sorry, that last one came from a Rice and Yaconelli book.

If I were reinventing youth ministry (again), I don't think I'd
have to look too much further than Deuteronomy 6 for a game
plan. There are three things in particular that stand out in this
passage.

First, the spiritual formation of children wasn't reserved for the Sabbath day or for special times of corporate worship in the temple or synagogue; it was to take place in the daily routines of life and home. Six of the nine "ideas" (instructions) that Moses gave to the Israelites were to take place in the home. If we want to make sure that children and young people get the spiritual training they need, we must engage parents and families in youth ministry.

Second, the spiritual formation of children was the responsibility of not only the immediate family but the entire faith community. When Moses gave this command, it wasn't addressed just to moms and dads but to all of Israel. The priests, the rabbis and every adult member of the whole community were charged with the responsibility for passing on the faith to the next generation. If we want to create an environment where children and teenagers grow strong in their faith, we will need to become more of an intergenerational church where everyone learns from each other.

Third, the truth the Israelites were to pass on existed long before the children of Israel were born. They did not create it and they could not change it or improve upon it. Their only responsibility was to receive it, carry it with them, guard it with care, live their lives according to it and then finally pass it on to the next generation in the same condition they had received it themselves—much like runners in a relay race passing the baton from one to the next. The God they were to tell their children about was the God of Abraham, Isaac and Jacob. Likewise, we have the gospel of Jesus Christ, given to us in the Word of God and preserved and preached by the church for generations, which now must be faithfully passed on to our children in its completeness and without compromise.

ENGAGING PARENTS

Reinvented youth ministry therefore has to begin by taking parents and families seriously. There have been many voices in recent years calling for youth workers to engage parents; those voices are only becoming more numerous, more persistent and a whole lot louder.

But as many youth workers know, partnering with parents in youth ministry is not an easy thing to do. Over twenty years ago I thought a really good parent seminar would do the trick, but after doing more than a thousand of them I now know they are not the answer, nor is any kind of program. I believe that partnering with parents is a completely new way of thinking about youth ministry altogether. It takes into consideration the input and involvement of parents with almost everything we do. How can this meeting or activity help parents? How can I include some parents in this? Is this strengthening or weakening the family? What can I do to help my students better understand their parents? What can I do to help parents better understand their kids? There are dozens of questions just like these that we can ask about everything we do in youth ministry. Remember, parents are the primary influencers of their kids—all the way through their high school years—so it only makes sense that we should be leveraging that influence as much as we possibly can.

The crazy thing is, neither we nor parents can do it alone. Top-notch parents are well aware of this truth. They take advantage of the help they can get from resources and people within their faith communities (including youth workers) without abdicating their own parental responsibility for their children's spiritual formation. Just as most of the spiritually mature young people I've met have had spiritually responsible parents at home, most of the spiritually responsible parents I've met have sought to become engaged or involved in some way in the youth ministry of the church.

Let me offer an object lesson to illustrate. Whenever anything breaks around my house, I usually go straight for the epoxy I keep in my garage. It's stronger than any other glue on the market, guaranteed. The interesting concept behind epoxy is that it really doesn't exist until you create it. You buy a kind of epoxy kit which consists of two tubes of gooey stuff: light-colored gooey stuff called resin and dark-colored gooey stuff called hardener. When you mix them together, you get a chemical reaction of some kind which turns the combined gooeyness into a substance that will soon become hard as steel. I'm not a rocket scientist, I admit, but I'm always kind of amazed by how two elements which by themselves don't stick to anything, combine to become something else entirely—the world's strongest bonding agent. I've used it to fix motors, musical instruments, bicycles, bricks, even fishing poles.

Something like the chemical reaction that creates epoxy is what happens when we form a partnership between youth ministers and parents. The youth ministry can't do it on its own. Neither can parents. But mix them together and I believe something amazing can happen. Let's face it, youth ministry is struggling right now. With all of our programs and personnel, we have not been very successful in bonding emerging generations to the Christian faith. Parents are also struggling. The stability of the family has eroded so much that many young people are wary of starting one of their own. The divorce rate continues to climb, making it almost impossible to argue that heterosexual marriage is more successful than same-sex marriage or any other kind of committed relationship.

And yet the church and the family are two of the most powerful and important institutions on the earth, both of them ordained by God to preserve and pass on the faith to each generation. If we can get them working together in harmony, kids are not only going to be more likely to adopt the faith of their parents but hang onto it long after they leave home.

I'm not talking about just becoming a profamily church. Some "family values" have become divisive political issues which have only served to alienate more young people from the church. This isn't about politics or fighting battles with people who do not share our commitment to the family. This is about affirming and strengthening the families we have in our churches and teaching them how to pass on their faith and values to their children. If we don't do that well, none of the legislation and political changes that we want will matter much anyway.

It's unfortunate that while we claim to believe in the family in our churches, we really don't do very much to help individual families succeed at home. Over the years I've found that church leaders get really nervous about *meddling* in the personal lives of fellow church members. As a result, we sometimes have no idea what's really going on in their homes or how we can help them during difficult times. I have served in churches which as a matter of policy essentially ignored families who were struggling with their marriages, were incapable of meeting their financial obligations, were neglecting the proper education or supervision of their children, or were disciplining them in a manner which could only be classified as borderline abuse. I know that getting involved in someone's family life can get complicated and is fraught with danger, but I don't believe that the Bible ever makes a distinction between our personal lives and our lives as members of the church.

The church and the family are indelibly linked and entirely dependent upon each other. When one part of the body hurts, the whole body does too (1 Corinthians 12:26). I'm not saying that we should interfere in people's lives against their will or cause people to be embarrassed or shamed because they have less than perfect families. Truth is, all families are dysfunctional, even the ones we read about in the Bible. Family life is messy, parenting is difficult, and the only people who believe differently are liars or authors of parenting books.

When I first started promoting junior high ministry about forty years ago, I remember hearing plenty of moans and groans from youth workers who really didn't want to have to work with "children." It took a long time before junior high ministry (now middle school ministry) became accepted and recognized as a significant part of the youth ministry landscape.

Likewise, I've found that many youth workers have had a hard time wrapping their arms around the concept of including parents and families in youth ministry. Here are just a few of the obstacles we have to overcome.

A negative image of parents. When I do seminars for youth workers on parent ministry, I sometimes play a little word association game with them: "What word or phrase first comes to mind when you think about parents of teenagers?" It's not uncommon to hear words like *incompetent, clueless, out-of-touch, bad examples, overly critical, controlling, abusive,* and so on. The game reveals some serious stereotypes that understandably discourage youth workers from getting involved with parents. Who wants to work with people who are clueless and incompetent?

If we are going to have an effective ministry to parents, we'll need to honor them, not criticize or stereotype them. Teens themselves like to perpetuate the my-parent-is-an-idiot mythology; we sometimes encourage and reinforce it with our jokes and parent slurs. As youth workers, we should be encouraging and blessing parents, holding them up in a positive light.

The assumption that teens don't want their parents to be involved. One study asked teenagers, "What, if anything, would you like to change about your family?" The most common response was "I wish I was closer to my parents." When they were asked, "Why aren't you closer to them right now?" most replied, "I don't know how."[2] Our youth ministries can help both parents and teens learn how to be closer to each other.

A fear of parents. I conducted an Understanding Your Teenager seminar at a church recently and before the seminar, the youth pastor looked at all the parents who were there and said, "I don't think I've met most of these people." I asked him, "Why not?" He said, "Well, meeting parents just gets me out of my comfort zone."

He's not alone. There are many youth workers who have a difficult time meeting parents, let alone helping them. Maybe like the teens they work with, they just don't know how to relate to parents. Maybe they have an irrational fear of them or just don't have the time. But whatever the reason, the very idea of working with parents strikes fear and loathing into the hearts of many youth workers. This is a serious obstacle to overcome.

The belief that things are just fine the way they are. When I point out that we've got problems in youth ministry, some frustrated youth pastors get a little defensive. "Who are you to tell me that my ministry isn't effective the way it is?" It's not easy for youth workers to admit that youth ministry might not be working. After all, everything looks pretty good on the surface. The church has invested a ton of money in youth ministry, the kids are coming and the programs are humming right along. From the point of view of a youth pastor, life is good. "I like working with kids and I know that God has called me to do this."

I acknowledge that most youth pastors and most youth ministries are getting some good results and doing a lot of good. But we can get better, and the consensus is growing that one of the most effective things we can do to get better is to engage parents.

The bad reputation of family ministry. Just like "family entertainment," "family ministry" can have a rather unexciting sound to a youth pastor. "Just don't call me a family pastor" is what I hear from youth workers who are considering the pros and cons of adding parents to their ministry responsibilities. "I think I'd rather watch the grass grow."

But a youth ministry that includes parents is not for the faint of heart. It can be just as innovative and creative and risky as youth ministry. In fact it's the next frontier in church ministry and therefore will require some of the most out-of-the-box thinking that we've done in a long time in the church. It will be anything but dull.

It's just one more thing to add to an already busy schedule. Mark DeVries notes that many youth workers avoid working with parents because it becomes just one more plate to spin: "But because we can't possibly keep all the plates spinning, youth ministry at its best involves a continual process of setting and adjusting priorities, of deciding what we will wring our hands about and what we will let slide. And let's face it, ministry to or through parents of teenagers has simply been one of the many things on our to do list that we've had to let slide."[3]

Actually a partnership with parents will probably result in less activity, not more. If we know that by helping parents we can impact the thousands of hours they spend with their own kids, then we can cut a few hours of youth group programming to focus on spending our time encouraging and equipping them to succeed with their kids.

The assumption that youth workers are too young. This can be a legitimate concern, depending of course on the age of the youth worker. I would have to agree that some youth workers *are* in fact too young to be effective with parents, at least when it comes to understanding the issues parents face and relating to them as peers. That's very difficult for a twentysomething youth worker to do. I know I had no idea what it was like to be parent of a teenager until I became one.

But youth workers can be a tremendous resource and blessing to parents even when they are much younger. Youth workers who are willing to learn how to relate to adults as well as they relate to teenagers will have no problem establishing credibility and trust with parents. In areas of obvious weakness, such as providing parenting advice, older adults or grandparents in the church can become excellent mentors for parents.

Misperceptions regarding results. For many youth workers, results are comfortably measured in attendance figures, number (or quality) of programs and events, conversions, decisions, baptisms and the like. Goals like those can be reasonably achieved with the right combination of people, programs and hard work. But ministry to and with parents changes the rules of the game quite a bit, making youth workers very uneasy. How will results be measured? Can they be measured at all?

Truth is, results will be not only measurable but they should be considerably better and more meaningful than those of the past. More and more pastors (and the churches they serve) are now realizing that youth ministry is not about short-term results but those which produce fruit in the lives of kids long after they leave our youth groups. It's easy to achieve short-term outcomes with a program, but to get long-term outcomes, a long-term strategy is required. We may never know exactly what our efforts to help parents will produce, but we have every reason to believe that our efforts will not be in vain.

A FEW BABY STEPS

Where to start?

First, *create a mission or vision statement which clearly articulates a commitment to parents and families.* I have to admit that if anyone had asked me forty years ago for my youth ministry mission or vision statement I wouldn't have had a clue what they were talking about. We really didn't think too much about what we were doing or why we did it in those days. But now, thanks to people like Steven Covey and Doug Fields, we all have mission statements.

What I've found a bit curious, however, is that as much as parent ministry gets talked about these days in youth ministry circles, I haven't found in any youth ministry books too many suggestions on how to write youth ministry mission statements which include working with parents, supporting families or integrating kids into the life of the church. I visited a popular youth ministry website recently which listed a sampling of more than fifty youth ministry purpose statements submitted by readers. Not even one of them included an acknowledgment of the important role that parents and families play in the spiritual formation of teenagers.[4] Here's a pretty typical youth ministry mission statement:

> [Our youth ministry] exists to reach teenagers for Christ and to make disciples of them by teaching God's Word, building community and involving students in mission and service.

If I were a parent, I would gladly drop my kids off at this youth group so that those youth leaders could do this job for me. But that's not what we want to communicate to parents. By contrast, here's a mission statement with a little different emphasis:

[Our youth ministry] exists to reach teenagers for Christ and to make disciples of them by encouraging parents, teaching God's Word, building community and involving families in mission and service.

It's not a big change but a small baby step that communicates a completely different attitude toward parents and families. Of course youth ministry mission statements don't mean much unless they parallel the mission and vision of the church. If the church has a vision for partnering with the family and becoming more intergenerational, then a youth ministry vision for partnering with families and including young people in the church community is likely to get some traction. If the church doesn't expect you to work with parents, however, or to involve young people in the life of the church, then any vision that includes those things is likely to be dead on arrival.

Like I said, this is not a youth ministry issue, it's a church issue. All the ministries of the church should be pulling in the same direction—the children's ministry, the family ministry, the education ministry, the men's ministry, the women's ministry, the evangelism and missions ministries—they should all be helping parents and supporting families just as the youth ministry is doing. If your church is not this kind of church, remember that churches can change and I believe that young people are in a better position to bring about change than anybody. It comes slowly and one step at a time.

Second (and this may sound a bit obvious), *acknowledge that all kids have parents.* I've found that it's tempting in youth ministry to treat teenagers as if they have no parents at all. This is particularly true with high school students. But unless your have kids in your group who are living on their own (which you probably don't), you can take the number of kids in your group, multiply by two and that's how many parents are probably connected to your youth ministry in some way. As Mark DeVries notes, "We're foolish to make changes which affect our young people without first consulting the people who are most invested in them. They are our senior partners, the ones who'll be doing ministry with 'our kids' long after we're gone."[5]

I know that some kids may come to your youth ministry without their parents. Or you may have some kids whose parents are divorced, dead or have otherwise disappeared from their kids' lives. That's OK. Don't let those kids set the agenda for your whole church or youth ministry. You can deal with those situations as they present themselves and find caring adults who will come alongside those kids.

Some church youth workers tell me that they are reaching so many nonchurched kids that most of the kids in their youth ministry don't have Christian parents. My short answer to that one is simply: *make those parents part of your mission field*. Obviously, a youth ministry that is reaching nonchurched kids should also be evangelizing nonchurched parents. Parents are likely to be very responsive to the gospel when they notice a positive change in the lives of their kids. I know many parents who have been led to Christ by their teen children.

Third, *think of every parent as a partner in youth ministry*. They don't all have to be great parents or those who are willing to serve in the youth ministry. All parents, even those who don't come to your church, can be partners. Start with those who are willing or who are already doing it and things will grow out from there. Remember, the more you include and involve parents in your youth ministry, the more likely you will be to influence the hearts and minds of their kids forever. One day, inevitably, the kids in your youth ministry are going to leave. You may be able to stay connected with some of them for a while, but not most of them and even then, for not very long. Parents, on the other hand, will be there for their kids through their college years, graduations, weddings, holidays, even helping their children raise their grandkids. And the cycle repeats itself. This is lifelong, multigenerational influence that youth workers can't possibly have on their own. By engaging parents and helping them do what they do best, you impact kids in ways you could never do otherwise.

Fourth, *let parents be parents*. Our goal is not to turn parents into youth workers, although some parents may want to get involved as youth leaders and serve on your team of volunteers. That's fine if they do, but what we really want to do is to leverage the immense amount of influence that they already have in their own homes. Every home can become an extension of the youth ministry, and the youth ministry can be an extension of the home. You can work together with parents to make disciples of their kids. Wouldn't it be great if everything you were teaching in your youth ministry was being reinforced and put into practice at home? It can happen by supporting parents as much as we expect them to support us, and by teaching kids to honor and respect their parents.

> By engaging parents and helping them do what they do best, you impact kids in ways you could never do otherwise.

Fifth, *go slow*. Don't push too hard. If you do, this will just become another discouraging thing in the lives of parents, one more indicator that they aren't "good" parents. Again, start with a few who are willing to get more involved in the spiritual training of their kids or already are and let them help you get things off the ground. Take a slow, steady approach, keeping in mind that this is a serious paradigm shift that may take years to bring to fruition.

Sixth, *provide parents with some tools.* You don't want to just nag parents about being better parents. All that does is produce guilt and frustration because most parents really don't know what to do. I was conducting a parent seminar at a church recently, and I asked parents to share some ideas for family devotions. Not only did they not have any ideas to share, most of those parents had no idea what I meant by the term "family devotions." It became clear to me that these parents were in desperate need of some practical tools for teaching and training their children at home. Sometimes just a simple thing like a list of questions to ask their kids after a youth group meeting can be a powerful resource that will help them get more involved in the spiritual formation of their children.

> Every home can become an extension of the youth ministry, and the youth ministry can be an extension of the home.

ENGAGING THE CONGREGATION

We've had to go to great effort to make the church as segregated as it is today. Churches are naturally intergenerational by definition, one of the last places on earth where people can actually still have an intergenerational experience. Where else do entire families go together on any kind of regular basis? Some families don't even know how to do dinner together anymore, but they still go to church.

So it seems rather incredible that when they get to church we deliberately separate everybody from each other. We send the adults one way and the children another. You know the drill: younger children go to the children's ministry building (or the nursery), teens to the youth ministry building, while mom and dad make themselves comfortable in the adult service, not having to do what my parents had to do most of their adult lives—make their kids behave in church.

I can't tell you how many times I had to be disciplined by my parents for passing notes, chewing gum, drawing or playing drums on the hymnbooks, kicking the pew in front of me, shooting spit wads or begging to go to the bathroom for the third time in twenty minutes. I'm not suggesting that forcing kids to sit through dull and boring church services is a great way to raise children up in the nurture and admonition of the Lord, but I am always amazed by how much I actually did learn from years of hearing sermons and singing hymns and reciting creeds and listening to old people pray and give testimonies. Those people were all part of my family growing up. I gained much from my years of worshiping with my family and the rest of the congregation in "big people's church."

But now everyone pretty much does their own thing. You can find stand-alone programs for every age group, from birth through the golden years, at almost every church in town. I recently was invited to play banjo in a worship band (go figure) at a church in Southern California offering seven different worship services at the same time. Worshipers could choose the service to attend based on whether they preferred contemporary rock, edgy rock, pop, traditional hymns, smooth jazz, country or bluegrass. You can guess which service I was in. As I looked around the room, it was noticeably devoid of young people. No children at all. The church makes it very clear that their worship services are "for adults only" and oh yeah, please turn off your cell phones.

This is an extreme example of course, but in many if not most churches today, not only the youth feel unwelcome in adult services, but the older members (seniors) do as well. Like children and teenagers, they are often relocated to services of their own (the "traditional service"), or they are left with the difficult choice of finding another church that reminds them of the one they attended when they were younger.

Now that I've got my AARP card I can speak with some authority to the question of how older people in the church are treated. Fifty years ago, traditional churches seemed to be ignoring and neglecting their young. They were failing to respond to the needs of adolescent culture. That's why so many of us championed the cause of youth ministry in the local church during the 1960s and 1970s.

I realize that turnabout is fair play, but today we almost have the opposite problem. Many churches, in their efforts to be relevant and responsive to the needs of young adults (which may or may not include teenagers) have marginalized and abandoned their old folks.

Getting up in years myself, I can sympathize with some of the older people who just don't understand what's going on in their own churches. They feel lost. Certainly they feel out of place wearing dressy clothes to church when everyone else is in flip flops and jeans. I feel bad for elderly folks who come to church and finally just out of exhaustion have to sit down in the middle of a thirty-minute "worship set" with a look of embarrassment on their faces because they are physically unable to remain standing as long as the young people. No one gives them permission to do so.[6]

My aunt Mabel is ninety years old and doesn't go to church much anymore. She's perfectly capable and willing to go. At this writing, she's in relatively good health and sharp as a tack. But she no longer can find a church that feels anything like the church she remembers, where hymns are sung, testimonies are given and the Word of God is preached. The church she and her late husband helped to plant and grow in her home town now has a new name (one that cuts their denominational ties) and no longer meets in the sanctuary but in the new multipurpose room. The grand old sanctuary has been converted into a coffee house for the teenagers. The same pattern has been repeated in churches all over town, so aunt Mabel is content to stay home, watch Bill Gaither videos and read her King James Bible.

I'll soon be in my aunt Mabel's shoes, but that's not what bothers me. What bothers me is that the young people of the church are missing out on the incredible vitality and wisdom and spiritual strength of people like my aunt Mabel and other members of her generation who are no longer considered an important part of the church.

I think it's rather ironic that during a time when healthy progress is being made by churches to cooperate with each other and to do away with the kind of denominational labels that have separated Christians for years, that trend has not been mirrored in local congregations. Most churches today are either extremely age-segregated (like a shopping mall) or they target one particular age group to the exclusion of all the others. I know it's not easy to meet the needs of everyone at once. And with today's increased life expectancy, it's getting even harder. If your church represents a good cross-section of your community, you probably have five, maybe even six generations in attendance.[7] That's compared to just three or four generations that was more typical a hundred years ago. There are definitely going to be obstacles and challenges, but as Michael Horton puts it, "We are not builders, boomers, busters or emergent but a communion of saints."[8] We should be demonstrating that in more than just words.

Most of us can agree that the church is supposed to be a true faith community, undivided by rich or poor, male or female, black or white, saint or sinner, young or old. There really aren't any biblical or theological arguments that can be made for a church that doesn't include a healthy cross section of the community where it is located—all races, all genders, all walks of life, all age groups growing together, serving together and worshiping together in unity. Certainly this was in the mind of Jesus when he prayed "that all of them may be one, Father, just as you are in me and I am in you. May they also be in us so that the world may believe that you have sent me" (John 17:21).

I suppose many people in the church would argue that we can have unity even though we don't all worship together or meet together. We're all part of the same church family. But just as family can't be all split up and still call itself a family, the church can't be all split up and still call itself a church. We are either the family of God or we're not.

Earlier I wrote about how the invention of adolescence as a separate stage of life led to the infantilizing of teenagers. It also led to their isolation from the adult population. By labeling teenagers as "not-adults," adults were in a sense given permission to distance themselves from adolescents. They no longer had anything in common with them. That's why young people have had to create their own anti-adult culture—with its own language, music and customs. That's also why youth ministry was called into existence by God. I believe that God responded to this shift in culture by calling thousands of men and women to come alongside teenagers to stem the tide of abandonment and to keep them connected to their families and the church.

Think about this: *If I were the devil—and if I wanted to destroy the Christian faith—how would I do it?* Quite honestly I can't think of a better way than to put as much distance as possible between children and the adults who care about them the most, especially their parents. If it's true that the Christian faith is only one generation away from extinction, then any disconnect between the generations will surely undermine one generation's ability to pass faith on to the next.

There's a growing consensus that most of the emotional and behavioral problems we see among teenagers—like suicide, substance abuse, depression, sexual promiscuity, disrespect for authority and so on—have as their root cause the abandonment of teenagers not only by the significant adults in their lives but by the institutions which in the past might have provided for them a place of safety and refuge.

I've heard today's teenagers described as *a tribe apart, a generation alone, all grown up with no place to go* and other terms which describe their isolation from adults. After several years of interviewing teenagers, author Patricia Hersch wrote, "A clear picture of adolescents, of even our own children, eludes us—not necessarily because they are rebelling, or avoiding or evading us. *It is because we aren't there.* Not just parents, but any adults. . . . The most stunning change for adolescents today is their aloneness."[9] In his book *Hurt,* veteran youth worker Chap Clark agrees: "The young have not arrogantly turned their backs on the adult world. Rather, they have been forced by a personal sense of abandonment to band together and create their own world—separate, semisecret, and vastly different from the world around them."[10] Abandonment, he says is the "defining characteristic of adolescents."[11]

I've seen this developing for years and have been encouraging youth workers especially to stem the tide of abandonment by helping to bring the generations together again. We should strive to be solution to the problem of abandonment rather than a contributor to it. But regrettably too many of our youth groups isolate teenagers further from the adults they need to be around the most. At the very time in their lives when they need adult mentors and role models, we warehouse them in youth groups with their own teaching, their own social events, their own mission trips, even their own worship services. They rarely interact with the adult population of the church at all, except for those few adults who are willing to give up their own place in the adult church to become part of the youth ministry.

ATTEMPTS AT REINTEGRATION

The adults who volunteer with their churches' youth programs are heroic and provide a remarkable demonstration of incarnational ministry, but I'm not sure this sort of sacrifice should be expected of adult volunteers. There are plenty of ways for caring adults to come alongside kids without giving up their own opportunities for spiritual growth and participation in the life of the church.

To be quite honest, I've found that youth ministry often attracts adult volunteers who (1) themselves don't have a high view of the church, (2) are not themselves growing spiritually or (3) don't seem to have any friends their own age. Don't get me wrong, I have great admiration and respect for people who sacrifice their time and get out of their comfort zones to do youth ministry as a volunteer. We need a lot more of them for sure. But I believe there is a better way to bring youth and adults together than by segregating youth from adults and then trying to get adults to come over to the other side. I don't think Jesus was praying in John 17 for something that he knew would be impossible.[12]

We either believe what Jesus said or we don't. His prayer for unity was a missional prayer. "May they be one . . . so that the whole world might believe you sent me" (John 17:21). He told his disciples, "All men will know that you are my disciples, if you love one another" (John 13:35). An intergenerational church can be a powerful and prophetic witness to the reconciling and uniting power of the gospel. The church should be challenging rather than adopting the destructive trends in society which isolate people from each other, infantilize youth and discriminate against the elderly.

Certainly the church has been called to be in the world and engaging culture, but it should also be providing a model, a demonstration or at least a glimpse into what the kingdom of God is all about. We should be doing things differently in the church from how they are done in the world. While the world elevates the rich and the powerful, we elevate the poor and the weak as Jesus taught us to do. While the world promotes a culture of narcissism and greed, we encourage a posture of humility and self-sacrifice. While the world honors the impressive and the large, we honor the unimpressive and the small. And while the world abandons and marginalizes young people by driving a wedge between the young and the old, we come alongside our young people and give them a place of significance by bringing the generations together again. That should be one of the primary goals of youth ministry. The church should be the one place left in the world where the young and the old can coexist and have fellowship with each other.

In San Diego where I live, there are several churches which are well-known for attracting young people. Their worship centers—with theatre-style seating, state-of-the-art sound and lighting—rival anything you would find at the top concert venues and night clubs in town. Services feature loud, professionally presented music on brightly-lit stages with fog machines and celebrity pastors who chat with the audience much like a late-night TV talk show host. It's not uncommon to see Twitter feeds popping up on the side screens along with song lyrics and ads for church-related events and resources. All of this is truly impressive and obviously very effective with people who expect state-of-the-art communication technology.

But when I look around the room I notice that I'm the only one with gray hair. There are plenty of bald heads, but most of them are intentionally bald. I don't mind at all being the oldest person in the room, but I wonder, is this a church? I understand completely the need to do missionary work—to identify people groups and find ways to communicate effectively with them. But once people become part of the family of God, shouldn't they be introduced to the church in all its intergenerational glory?

Traditional churches can become more untraditional in order to include emerging generations, and "emerging" churches can learn to include and affirm the meaningful traditions of the past to connect with older generations. We can teach our older brothers and sisters in Christ to accept young people with their tattoos, piercings, strange clothes and postmodern ideas. We can likewise teach our young people to love and appreciate their elders with their bad haircuts, walkers, hearing aids and foggy memories about how everything used to be. This will not be easy and it won't done quickly. It won't look very impressive. It will be difficult and messy just like families are difficult and messy.

Mike Yaconelli and I didn't always agree on everything, but we definitely saw eye to eye on this issue. He once wrote the following:

> Youth group is good. But there's a better good. It's called church. Not youth church, or contemporary church, or postmodern church. Just plain, boring, ordinary church. Yes, that's right. Church. The place were people who don't know each other get to know each other; where people who don't normally associate with each other associate; where people who are different from each other learn how to be one.

Mostly church is the place were we can grow old together. And it turns out that growing old together is still the best way to bring lasting results with students. Growing old together is where we teach (and learn from) each other what discipleship means in the everyday world.[13]

MORE BABY STEPS

It's possible to be an intergenerational church and still have a youth group. There are many youth activities which have their time and place. But let me offer a few questions I think youth workers should always ask about every youth meeting or activity:

- Is this really necessary?
- Will this meeting or activity do more good than harm?
- Is there a way for us to do this meeting or activity so that other age groups in the church will also be included or involved?

I know those questions don't always have easy answers, but they are questions that aren't often asked by anyone. There are so many things that we do which aren't really necessary or beneficial for our kids. We have a tendency to do them because they have "always" been done and that's what everyone expects will be done.

A good example of what I'm talking about is the practice of many churches to conduct youth worship services. I acknowledge that times of authentic worship are wonderful for kids. I'm not opposed to youth worship in general, so that's not my point. But what I find astonishingly troublesome is the common practice of providing a regular worship service for teenagers which becomes for them an alternative to the corporate worship of the church.

I visit quite a few youth ministries around the country and I've found that even small churches feel obligated these days to provide a special worship service for teenagers on Sunday morning. This service is typically held prior to the adult worship service or at some other time when the youth can attend. Most of the time this is not officially sanctioned as a substitute for the regular corporate worship service, as the youth are encouraged to attend the regular adult worship as well. But I've found that in many churches, the youth rarely attend the adult services or they do so with little enthusiasm. Usually they only attend because their parents make them go.

Providing a youth worship service may seem harmless, even beneficial, but when we train teenagers to believe that the regular worship service of their church is inadequate both in style and content, we undermine not only the unity of the church and its traditions, but the possibility that they will ever return to the church when they grow too old for the youth group.

I spoke recently with the youth pastor from a megachurch who told me that his church now requires him to conduct youth worship service concurrently with all of the adult worship services in order to *free up seats* for visitors in the main sanctuary. I couldn't believe I was hearing this. Needless to say this is an example of age-segregation at its worst. Sacrificing the youth of the church for potential visitors seems to me an outrageously bad trade-off.

Sure, there are times when students need times of instruction and fellowship and ministry which is especially suitable for teenagers. There is still a need to occasionally provide socials and fun times just for teenagers. I still have fond memories of my junior high Sunday school class taught by Mrs. Baughman and I loved going to summer camp because it gave me a rare opportunity to be on my own for a week. It was at camp at age thirteen when I gave my life to Jesus, an especially significant decision for me because I made it alone and not just to please my parents.

For many teenagers, the youth group can feel a little bit like having to sit at the "kids' table" at Thanksgiving dinner. It was usually a card table with some folding chairs around it. As a teenager, I still remember how good it felt to be included at the dining room table with all the adults in my family. It was a huge affirmation for me—not to mention that it gave me easy access to second helpings. I watched my table manners just so that I wouldn't get sent back down. More often than not, the kids' table turned into a food fight.

When I was a youth pastor, we tried seating the teenagers together in the balcony of the church during worship services. You can guess what happened. When you have a group of teens together in one place with few adults around, you can almost count on a food fight breaking out. But if you seat those same teenagers throughout the sanctuary, right alongside the adults, most teenagers can be surprisingly well behaved and engaged in what is going on.

If there is a men's ministry in your church, the young men who are still in their teens should be welcome to participate. Likewise the women's ministry should find ways to connect young women in their teens with the older women of the church. The missions department can plan family mission trips and all kinds of outreach opportunities that are intergenerational in nature. I submit that there are few church programs which cannot bring the generations together and become more effective in the process.

I love what one church did for its Sunday morning "preworship" hour. The church offers numerous classes for youth and adults not divided by age categories but by topics which change every few weeks. All church members are encouraged to sign up for the topics they want until the classes are full, not really knowing who their classmates will be. Admittedly the topics themselves often group people by age or their particular interest, but surprisingly some classes end up with both teens and senior citizens in the same room. According to the seniors, their classes have never been so lively!

I have worked with middle-schoolers now for more than forty years, and whenever I welcome new students into the church's youth ministry, I tell them that they have just become part of a great big old dysfunctional family.

> You're going to discover that you have some grandpas, grandmas, uncles and aunts you never knew you had. It's called the church. There are people here who will get to know you, show up for you, pray for you and care about what happens to you. They are your older brothers and sisters in Christ. You are part of their family and they are part of yours. You can access these people for free and anytime you want!

This is a message that I have found kids love to hear. They really want it to be true. So do we. We've tried to implement programs to encourage this in many ways over the years, including a prayer partners ministry which enlists older members of the congregation to pray for our students on a variety of levels—ranging from praying for them on a "secret pal" basis to mentoring them one on one. Like any initiative, this has required patience, but I believe it's possible to retrain the church to accept and encourage its youth and give them a seat at the adult table.

It has taken youth ministry almost fifty years to get where we are today. Perhaps we can, in a somewhat shorter amount of time, back things up and restore the intergenerational quality of the church that we have lost. You see, what I'm calling for as a new way of doing youth ministry or doing church isn't new at all. For hundreds of years, the church was intergenerational and family-based. Somehow in the process of getting youth ministry established in the church, we undermined the unity of the church which now must be restored.

We can't turn the clock back of course, nor should we. Youth ministry has done a tremendous amount of good and that good should remain. But perhaps now we can make the kind of course corrections that will bring healing and unity back to our churches once again.

This may be stating the obvious, but an intergenerational church and an intergenerational approach to youth ministry will probably be more achievable in smaller churches than in larger ones. This is not always the case, but small churches definitely have the advantage here. In the past, small churches tried to act like large churches. I think the challenge today is for large churches to act like small churches. It can be done. There are several large churches which have provided us with some hopeful models of what a church can look like when it prioritizes families and programs with a more intergenerational mindset.[14]

Some youth workers feel hesitant to move toward an intergenerational approach because they are worried they will work themselves out of a job. If that were to happen, I would just say congratulations. You've been successful! Whether or not you have a job is not really the point of youth ministry or any kind of ministry for that matter. If your primary concern is keeping your job, you probably need to go find another one anyway.

The invention of adolescence spawned a multibillion-dollar industry, which of course is now completely dependent upon it.

A recent PBS television special titled "The Merchants of Cool" gave a revealing glimpse into how huge corporations market the latest fads, fashions and values to teenagers for the purpose of relieving teenagers of the considerable amount of disposable cash they have in their pockets.[15] These entertainment, clothing and media empires have a vested interest in perpetuating the isolation and extension of adolescence for as long as they can. I would hope that the invention of youth ministry hasn't spawned an industry that perpetuates the isolation of teenagers from the rest of the church.

MOVING ON

It has now been more than fifteen years since I walked away from Youth Specialties and began a new ministry to parents. Understanding Your Teenager certainly hasn't had as much publicity or financial success, but it has been my joy. It has allowed me to encourage thousands of youth workers to become more engaged with parents and to equip almost a million parents who have attended our seminars to stay connected to their teens and remain faithful to their awesome and holy responsibility to raise their kids up in the Lord.

I probably didn't realize it then, but I know now that I was part of something very special with the creation of Youth Specialties. Mike and I—along with many others who joined with us and even competed against us—helped grow a youth ministry industry which literally didn't exist before we put together that first *Ideas* book over forty years ago. During our lifetime we witnessed an unprecedented rise in the number of youth workers in the church, increased validation for the profession of youth ministry and an explosion of resources, education, technology and systems to help us all do it better.

There are some who have suggested that an apology is in

order but I disagree. There is nothing we could have accomplished at Youth Specialties without the providential permission and blessing of God who called all of us to do what we do. Hindsight is always 20/20, and certainly there are things we learned *not* to do along the way. But I'm grateful that somehow I was allowed to play a small role in the much bigger story of youth ministry—which isn't over by a long shot. There is still plenty of great youth work yet to be done.

I've been asked how I would feel as the cofounder of Youth Specialties, if YS were to just fold up its tents and call it quits. No more conventions, no more youth ministry seminars, no more books and magazines specifically for youth workers. Personally I don't expect that any of that that will happen anytime soon. But *if it did* . . .

- because parents were taking so much responsibility for passing the faith on to their kids
- and because churches had become so accustomed to including young people in all the ministries of the church
- and because church ministry conferences included so much help and encouragement for youth workers that special youth ministry organizations and training events were no longer needed

If it did because of all those things, then I think we all of us could say "mission accomplished."

ONE (MORE) THING

After I left in 1994, Youth Specialties grew rapidly and prospered well into the first decade of the twenty-first century. But a few years after Mike's death in 2003, the company was sold to its long-time publishing partner, Zondervan Publishing House—a division of HarperCollins and News Corporation, the second-largest media conglomerate in the world (behind the Walt Disney Company). Youth Specialties was expecting to benefit from the financial assets and expertise of Zondervan, and Zondervan was expecting continued growth of its Youth Specialties product line with the conferences and events serving as a marketing bonanza.

By the end of the decade, however, increased competition and a growing economic recession severely impacted attendance at the National Youth Workers Convention as well as the other YS event-based ministries, leading Zondervan to downsize and divest itself of all but its publishing interest. Almost all of the YS staff in El Cajon, California, including president Mark Oestreicher, were let go. The company was sold to a Minnesota nonprofit ministry called YouthWorks, best known for its short-term mission trips involving thousands of youth and families each year. I have to admit that I was not familiar at all with YouthWorks or the people behind it, but by all accounts they are committed to keeping the legacy and mission of Youth Specialties alive well into the future.[1] I'm anxious to see what these two ministries will be able to accomplish together.

Let me wrap up this book by saying that the legacy and mission of Youth Specialties—indeed the legacy and mission of all of us engaged in youth ministry—is to be faithful to the truth, the good news of the gospel, which has been delivered to us by our parents and grandparents and must likewise be passed on to our children and their children. After all, that's what compelled us to get into youth ministry in the first place. It's not about us. It's not even about teenagers. It's all about Jesus Christ and the incredible sacrifice that he made for us on the cross. I'll say it again: reinvented youth ministry, no matter what it may look like in the future, absolutely must get it right on this issue.

It's a really old movie now, but I still love that scene in *City Slickers* where Billy Crystal's character, Mitch, is alone with Curly, played by Jack Palance. Curly is giving Mitch some life advice.

Curly: Do you know what the secret of life is? *[holds up one finger]* This.

Mitch: Your finger?

Curly: One thing. Just one thing. You stick to that and the rest don't mean s***.

Mitch: But, what is the "one thing"?

Curly: That's what you have to find out.

Toward the end of his life, the great Swiss-German theologian Karl Barth was asked by a student if he could summarize the most important theological discovery of his life. Barth answered without hesitation: "Jesus loves me, this I know; for the

Bible tells me so."[2] This was his *one thing*. When Moses gave his instructions to Israel in the *Shema* of Deuteronomy 6, they were not left guessing at what his *one thing* was. The fact that so few Christian young people today are able to articulate the content of their faith is a terrible indictment of the kind of youth ministry we have been doing in recent years.

There are many messages that we can communicate to kids, but only one that really matters in the end. It is the message of our redemption from sin, the loving sacrifice that Jesus made for us on the cross. If the young people who attend our youth groups aren't getting that message, then nothing we do really matters all that much.

I have enjoyed reading some of the new youth ministry books and resources being published today on how to help teenagers grow in their faith and become more passionate about following Jesus. It's wonderful that there is a new emphasis on social action and living like Jesus taught us to do. But good works are not the gospel. While good works flow out of our love for Jesus and what he did for us on the cross, good works do not necessarily lead one to faith in Christ. We must make sure that our teenagers know the Christ who died for their sins and that by putting their faith in him, they can have life to its fullest both now and in the life to come. Therein is our hope and joy. Without that, all the good works and wonderful experiences mean nothing at all.

New models of youth ministry advocating transformational youth ministry, contemplative youth ministry, presence-centered youth ministry and prophetic youth ministry provide a healthy corrective from the program-centered youth ministries of the past to a focus on personal spirituality. There is much to recommend in all of these approaches. But in some quarters there is a dangerous trend toward dialing down the proclamation of the good news (objective truth) in favor of personal experience (subjective truth).

We can't leave our young people at the threshold of faith without making sure they understand the *one thing* that makes our faith different from every other faith. This is not just about pushing students for decisions or memorizing creeds. It's not about the words. It's about encountering the Word, the Truth, the only One who is capable of transforming their lives forever.

I love to sing with today's worship leaders and I acknowledge that there are some wonderful new songs for worship being written these days. But I sure would love to sing a few more like this great hymn which was written more than three hundred years ago:

> Ask ye what great thing I know, that delights and stirs
>   me so?
> What the high reward I win? Whose the name I glory in?
> Jesus Christ, the crucified.
>
> This is that great thing I know; this delights and stirs me so:
> Faith in him who died to save, Him who triumphed o'er
>   the grave.
> Jesus Christ, the crucified.

NOTES

Introduction

[1]For a complete history of youth ministry, see Mark Senter, *When God Shows Up* (Grand Rapids: Baker Academic, 2009).

[2]According to a study conducted in 2007, 70 percent of young adults ages twenty-three to thirty say they stopped attending church between the ages of eighteen and twenty-two <www.lifeway.com/lwc/article_main_page/0%2C1703%2CA%25253D165949%252526M%25253D200906%2C00.html?>. See also Christian Smith with Melinda Lundquist Denton, *Soul Searching: The Religious and Spiritual Lives of American Teenagers* (New York: Oxford University Press, 2005), and Dan Kimball, *They Like Jesus but Not the Church* (Grand Rapids: Zondervan, 2007).

Chapter 1: A Long Night in Chicago

[1]Christian Smith with Melinda Lundquist Denton, *Soul Searching: The Religious and Spiritual Lives of American Teenagers* (New York: Oxford University Press, 2005), p. 261.

[2]George Barna, *Revolutionary Parenting* (Ventura, Calif.: Gospel Light, 2007), p. 12.

[3]Mark DeVries, *Sustainable Youth Ministry* (Downers Grove, Ill.: InterVarsity Press, 2008), p. 10.

[4]Merton P. Strommen and A. Irene Strommen, *Five Cries of Parents* (San Francisco: Harper and Row, 1985), p. 124.

[5]Mark DeVries, *Family-Based Youth Ministry* (Downers Grove, Ill.: InterVarsity Press, 1994).

[6]Ibid., p. 18.

[7]Even Youth Specialties has joined the movement in recent years, now offer-

ing parenting seminars of their own: "Real World Parents," conducted by a seminar team led by Mark Matlock. For more information, visit <www .realworldparents.com>.

[8]HomeWord is now affiliated with Azusa Pacific University's Center for Youth and Family Ministry. Visit <www.homeword.com> or <www.apu .edu/youthandfamily/> for more information.

Chapter 2: Growing Up Nazarene

[1]For one thing, it would now be considered a crime for a teacher to provide transportation for a student in his or her private automobile!

[2]"The label 'teenager' first appeared commonly in American culture about 1955." H. Stephen Glenn, Jane Nelson and Lynn Lott, *Positive Discipline for Teenagers* (Rocklin, Calif.: Prima Publishing, 1994), from the foreword.

[3]Lev Grossman, "Grow Up? Not So Fast," *Time*, January 24, 2005, pp. 44, 52.

[4]G. Stanley Hall, *Adolescence: Its Psychology and Its Relations to Physiology, Anthropology, Sociology, Sex, Crime, Religion and Education*, vol. 2 (New York: D. Appleton and Company, 1905), pp. xiii, x. Quoted in Robert Epstein, *The Case Against Adolescence* (Sanger, Calif.: Quill Driver, 2007), p. 121.

[5]Christian Smith with Melinda Lundquist Denton, *Soul Searching: The Religious and Spiritual Lives of American Teenagers* (New York: Oxford University Press, 2005), p. 120.

[6]I first heard about "the myth of the teenage werewolf" in Marie Winn, *Children Without Childhood* (New York: Penguin, 1984).

[7]Pete Thomas, "Zac Sunderland Completes Around the World Sail," *Los Angeles Times*, July 17, 2009. <http://www.latimes.com/sports/la-sp-zac-sun derland17-2009jul17,0,3460856.story?page=1>.

[8]Epstein, *Case Against Adolescence*, p. 5

[9]Bruce Narramore, *Adolescence Is Not an Illness* (Old Tappan, N.J.: Revell, 1980).

[10]From a song written by my brother Jim, "If I Didn't Have Love," copyright 1975 by Jim Rice.

[11]Epstein, *Case Against Adolescence*, p. 161.

Chapter 3: My First Youth Ministry Job

[1]This line by Jim Rayburn has been published in many books and journals, but my earliest recollection of this quotation is "It's a sin to bore a kid *with the gospel.*" I've asked several of my Young Life friends to verify this, and

most agree. Rayburn's point was that we sometimes take something very exciting (the gospel) and turn it into something very uninteresting to teenagers. That's a sin.

[2]Dictionary.com defines *hootenanny* as "(1) a social gathering or informal concert featuring folk singing and sometimes dancing; (2) an informal session at which folk singers and instrumentalists perform for their own enjoyment; (3) a thingumbob."

[3]Christian Smith with Melinda Lundquist Denton, *Soul Searching: The Religious and Spiritual Lives of American Teenagers* (New York: Oxford University Press, 2005), pp. 162-63.

[4]Smith with Denton, *Soul Searching*, p. 164.

[5]Michael Spencer, "The Coming Evangelical Collapse," *Christian Science Monitor,* March 10, 2009 <www.csmonitor.com/2009/0310/p09s01-coop.html>.

[6]Smith with Denton, *Soul Searching*, pp. 162-71, 258, 262.

[7]Ibid., p. 35.

[8]Whenever I preach to adults, actually, I just pretend that they are all teenagers. If I can communicate well enough for teenagers to understand, then the adults will probably get it too.

[9]Michael Horton, *Christless Christianity* (Grand Rapids: Baker Books, 2008), p. 20.

[10]Jeff Jarvis, *What Would Google Do?* (New York: Collins Business, 2009), p. 11.

[11]See especially Mike King, *Presence-Centered Youth Ministry* (Downers Grove, Ill.: InterVarsity Press, 2006).

[12]We recently found in a box of memorabilia an old reel-to-reel tape recording of our marriage, which we had transferred to digital format so that we could listen to it. Hearing those vows we spoke to each other so many years ago brings back all the feelings of intimacy we could ever hope to experience any other way. Likewise, when I hear the gospel proclaimed each week in a true service of worship, I can't help but be drawn into intimacy with Jesus every single time.

Chapter 4: The Birth of Youth Specialties

[1]An excerpt from Mike Yaconelli, "Campus Life Is Not Just a Name," a one-page handout included in the program booklet for Youth for Christ International Midwinter Convention, January 2-4, 1968.

[2]Campus Life actually had what was called their 2+2 club philosophy, which was that an "Impact" (outreach) meeting would be held twice a month, and

an "Insight" (for Christian kids only) meeting would be held on alternate weeks. *Impact* and *Insight* manuals were produced that summer for YFC, but Mike and I only worked on the *Impact* manual.

[3]We later found out that the mere act of printing the book was, in effect, a copyright. We eventually did file a copyright with the Library of Congress.

[4]Ben Patterson, "The Plan for A Youth Ministry Reformation," *Youthworker,* Fall 1984.

Chapter 5: Going Big Time

[1]For the next eight years, Youth Specialties was headquartered at 861 Sixth Avenue, Suite 411, in San Diego. Today that part of downtown San Diego is a tourist attraction known as the Gaslamp District.

[2]Joseph Bayly, president of David C. Cook Publishing, was a columnist for *Eternity* magazine and author of such books as *The Gospel Blimp* and *I Saw Gooley Fly*. He was a mentor and became a good friend to both Mike and me. He showed up at the convention wearing a shirt made from a potato sack. John MacArthur had been a popular speaker at youth camps around Southern California and had just begun pastoring his father's old church, Grace Community in Panorama City, California. Mel White was a professor of communications at Fuller Seminary who later became a ghostwriter for people like Jerry Falwell, Pat Robertson and Billy Graham before announcing that he was gay in 1994 and becoming a leader in the gay rights movement. Lyman Coleman was active in the Faith at Work movement and founded Serendipity House, a leader in the small-group movement. Jay Kesler was at the time the national Campus Life director for YFC and eventually became the organization's president and later president of Taylor University and an author on youth and family issues. Sonny Salsbury was a popular folk artist and youth worker in the Nazarene church. Ralph Carmichael was a film and TV composer who had become well known for his songs "He's Everything to Me" and "Pass It On."

[3]Later on, after our convention became financially successful, we established a $1,000 "Jack Young Award" that we presented to other entrepreneurs in ministry on Jack's behalf.

[4]There's no way of knowing exactly how many youth workers are currently employed, but *Group* magazine reports that according to their research,

there are currently 60,000 full-time (paid) youth workers and approximately 200,000 more volunteers who are leading their church's youth ministries (*Group,* Jan/Feb 2009, p. 50.

[5]Kara Powell, "Shift" youth ministry conference, April 24, 2009. She referenced preliminary research from a longitudinal study for Fuller Youth Institute's "College Transition Project." Students were asked, "Why do you go to youth group?" The #1 answer was "My youth leader."

[6]Mark Holmen, *Faith Begins at Home* (Ventura, Calif.: Regal Books, 2007), p. 149.

[7]See Wayne Rice, *Engaging Parents in Youth Ministry* (Cincinnati: Standard Publishing, 2009).

[8]Mark DeVries, *Sustainable Youth Ministry* (Downers Grove, Ill.: InterVarsity Press, 2008), p. 15

[9]Dan Kimball, *They Like Jesus but Not the Church* (Grand Rapids: Zondervan, 2007), p. 82.

[10]Hal Lindsey worked with students at UCLA and was the bestselling author of *The Late Great Planet Earth*. Larry Richards authored such books as *Youth Ministry in the Local Church* and *Creative Bible Teaching*. Larry Norman was a rock singer and darling of the Jesus Movement who attracted attention for his groundbreaking album *Upon This Rock* (Capitol Records). Randy Stonehill was a friend of Norman's who was just beginning his career as a Christian artist. Barry McGuire was a late addition to our program as he was introduced to us at the convention by Tony Salerno, a California youth worker who had recently led him to Christ. McGuire was best known for his work with the New Christy Minstrels and his hit record *Eve of Destruction*.

[11]Interestingly enough, YS has come under a good deal of criticism in recent years for continuing the edgy quality of the National Youth Workers Convention and made the decision in 2009 to avoid "hot button issues" in the future. According to then-president Mark Oestreicher, future conventions will have "more unifying 'big room' gatherings that celebrate what the diverse crowds—ranging from conservative evangelicals to mainline Protestants and Catholics—have in common: the gospel of Jesus Christ, a belief in God's power to transform lives, and a passion for developing young people of faith." Bobby Ross Jr., "Less Edgy Conferences," *Christianity Today* online edition, June 23, 2009 <www.christianitytoday.com/ct/2009/july/8.15.html>.

Chapter 6: Nailing It to the Door

[1]We paid nothing for the rights to *The Wittenburg Door*, published it at a loss for more than twenty years and then sold it to a group in Dallas for $1.

[2]*The Wittenburg Door* 1, June 1971, p. 10.

[3]I found Hemingway's quote recently at <www.teachablemoment.org/ideas/crapdetecting.html>.

[4]"Head in the Sand Award," *The Wittenburg Door* 4, December 1971, p. 22.

[5]Ibid.

[6]There's a growing body of evidence coming from researchers telling us that as teenagers grow too old for their youth groups, they are leaving the church for good. LifeWay Research reported in a widely-publicized study that approximately 70 percent of students leave the church after they graduate from high school. "LifeWay Research Uncovers Reasons Why 18 to 22 Year Olds Drop Out of Church" <www.lifeway.com/lwc/article_main_page/0,1703,A=165949&M=200906,00.html>.

[7]This is somewhat of a condensation of Dan Kimball's main points in *They Like Jesus but Not the Church* (Grand Rapids: Zondervan, 2007).

[8]Ibid., p. 16.

[9]From the Search Institute 1990 study "Effective Christian Education: A National Study of Protestant Congregations." See also Mark DeVries, *Sustainable Youth Ministry* (Downers Grove, Ill.: InterVarsity Press, 2008), p. 13.

[10]Brush Arbor went through several more personnel changes after I left, and had a successful career as a top "positive country" band led by my brother Jim.

Chapter 7: The Expansion of Youth Ministry

[1]Mark Oestreicher, *Youth Ministry 3.0* (Grand Rapids: Zondervan 2009), p. 88.

[2]Michael Cromartie, "What American Teenagers Believe: A Conversation with Christian Smith," *Books and Culture*, January/February 2005, pp. 10-11.

[3]Mark DeVries, *Family-Based Youth Ministry* (Downers Grove, Ill.: InterVarsity Press, 2004), p. 17.

[4]The website is Purpose-Driven Youth Ministry Community <www.pdymcommunity.org/?p=1722>, accessed January 27, 2010.

[5]Mark DeVries, "Getting (and Keeping) Parents on Your Team," *Group*, January 2, 2003, p. 48.

[6]Mini-rant: It's interesting to me that most teenagers assume that worship songs can only be sung standing up. As soon as somebody pulls out a guitar and starts the music, everyone rises to their feet and feels obligated to remain vertical until the musicians leave the stage. Most teenagers have no memory of doing it any other way. I can't say for sure, but I'm guessing that the current practice of standing during the music comes from rock concerts attended by boomers and their buster kids. I can still remember my first U2 concert in the mid 1980s, when a football stadium full of people were on their feet for the entire 2-1/2-hour show. I was somewhat amazed by the endurance of the audience, including myself.

[7]The G.I. or "Greatest" Generation (1906-1924), the "Silent" Generation (1925-1943), "Boomers" (1944-1962), "Busters" or "Generation X" (1963-1981), "Millennials" (1982-2000), and the Internet Generation or "Generation Z" (2001-present).

[8]Michael Horton, *Christless Christianity* (Grand Rapids: Baker Books, 2008), p. 210.

[9]Patricia Hersch, *A Tribe Apart* (New York: Fawcett Columbine, 1998), p. 19.

[10]Chap Clark, *Hurt* (Grand Rapids: Baker Academic, 2004), p. 44.

[11]Ibid.

[12]I once heard pastor Juan Carlos Ortiz make the statement at one of our National Youth Workers Conventions that "denominationalism is the great sin of the church." That statement struck a chord inside of me then that has been resonating ever since.

[13]Mike Yaconelli, *Getting Fired for the Glory of God* (Grand Rapids: Zondervan, 2008), pp. 92-93.

[14]A couple of examples: The Think Orange movement from North Point Community Church in Atlanta, Georgia, and the HomePointe program from Lake Pointe Church in Rockwall, Texas.

[15]*Frontline,* "The Merchants of Cool," first broadcast 27 February 2001 by PBS. Directed by Barak Goodman and written by Rachel Dretzin. Also available online at <www.pbs.org/wgbh/pages/frontline/shows/cool/>.

One (More) Thing

[1]According to a press release posted on the YouthWorks website, "This move realigns *YS* under the umbrella of the youth ministry-minded organization of *YouthWorks*, which honors the legacy of the *YS* founders, positions *YS* for new success and significantly expands the reach of the *Youth-*

Works family of ministries. *YouthWorks* currently operates in more than 80 U.S. cities and Canada and has served more than 400,000 participants through 10,000 churches. *YS* serves more than 10,000 churches and 100,000 youth ministry workers worldwide. '*Both* YouthWorks *and* Youth Specialties *were founded to serve the Church by serving youth,*' said *Youth-Works* founder and President Paul Bertelson. '*We are excited about the complementary aspects each offers and believe the acquisition will enhance both ministries*'" <www.youthworks.com/pdfs/YS/YWAcquiresYS.pdf>, accessed February 18, 2010.

[2]Joseph L. Mangina, *Karl Barth: Theologian of Christian Witness* (Louisville, Ky.: Westminster John Knox, 2004), p. 9.

ABOUT THE AUTHOR

Wayne Rice is currently Pastor to Generations at College Avenue Baptist Church in San Diego, California. He still works with middle-school kids, plays the banjo and conducts Understanding Your Teenager seminars. For more information visit <www.waynerice.com>.

DATE DUE

JUL 3 1 2014			